# CUT IT! FOLD IT! GLUE IT!

## Bible Story Paper Crafts

Anita Reith Stohs

Illustrated by Bill Clark

CONCORDIA PUBLISHING HOUSE • SAINT LOUIS

*For James and Daniel Safarik*
*Psalm 98:4*


3558 S. Jefferson Avenue, St. Louis, MO 63118-3968
Manufactured in the United States of America



4 5 6 7 8 9 10 11 12 12 11 10 09 08 07 06 05 04

# Contents

# A Note to Teachers and Parents

Children learn by doing. These paper crafts help children review frequently used Bible lessons. They also can be displayed in the classroom or home as reminders of the lesson. Use these projects as idea starters for you and your class. Additional suggestions are provided at the end of each activity. Adapt the paper projects to materials you have or to other lessons you want to teach and reinforce.

Above all, allow children to come up with their own unique interpretations of the paper craft. Don't expect them to produce carbon copies of either an illustration in the book or a sample craft you have made. Use the patterns in this book with children who are too young to draw their own shapes. Encourage older children who are able to draw to make their own shapes. God is creative, and we should encourage the development of creativity in our classroom activities.

## Kinds of Paper

You can choose many kinds of paper products to complete the projects in this book:

Bond paper
Construction paper
Crepe paper
Drawing paper
Lightweight cardboard
Metallic paper
Newspaper
Paper bags
Poster board
Tissue paper
Tracing paper
Wallpaper
Watercolor paper
Wrapping paper

OLD TESTAMENT

# Let There Be Light: Stained-Glass Window

## Bible Story

**Creation (Genesis 1)**

"Let there be light," God said, and it was so. If you shine a light through a prism, the light divides into the colors of the rainbow. Let your stained-glass window remind you of God's marvelous gifts of light and color.

## Materials

Black construction paper
Plate
Pencil
Scissors
Colored tissue paper
Rubber cement (or glue)
Hole punch
Yarn

## Directions

1. Use the plate to trace a circle on a piece of black construction paper. Cut it out.
2. Fold the circle in half. Then fold it again.
3. Beginning at the fold, lightly draw shapes to be cut out. Cut them out. Unfold the circle.
4. To fill in the holes in the circle, lightly trace the shapes on colored tissue paper. Cut each tissue-paper shape about ½" larger than the traced shape. Glue the tissue-paper shapes in place with rubber cement. (Use white glue with younger children.)
5. When finished, punch a hole through the circle's edge. Tie a piece of yarn through it. Hang your circle in a window as a sun catcher.

## Other Ideas

1. Fold the circle three times. Cut different patterns into the folds.
2. Cut a sun's rays in the outside edge of the circle. Fill with bright colors.
3. Cut a black circle. Fill the circle with pieces of colored construction paper.

# Thank God for Trees:
# Slit-and-Slide Stand-Ups

## Bible Story

**Creation (Genesis 1)**

God made all the trees in our beautiful world. What tree do you like best? Make a stand-up tree to remind you to thank God for His creation.

## Materials

Green construction paper
Pencil
Scissors
Markers

## Directions

**Asymmetrical trees**

1. Draw the outline of a tree on construction paper.
2. Draw a strip out from each side of the tree's base.
3. Cut out the tree. At one end of the strip, cut a slit a little more than halfway down. On the other end of the strip, cut a slit a little more than halfway up.
4. Write "Thank You, God, for (*name of tree*)" around the strip.
5. Slide the slits together to make the tree stand up.

## Other Ideas

Use slits to make stand-up people, objects, or landforms for other Bible stories.

**Symmetrical trees**

1. Fold a sheet of construction paper in half. Then fold it again.
2. Draw half of a tree on the fold. Cut out the trees.
3. Cut a slit a little more than halfway down from the top of one tree shape. Cut a second slit going a little more than halfway up from the bottom of the second tree shape.
4. Slide the slits together to make the tree stand up.
5. Write "Thank You, God, for (*name of tree*)" on the tree.

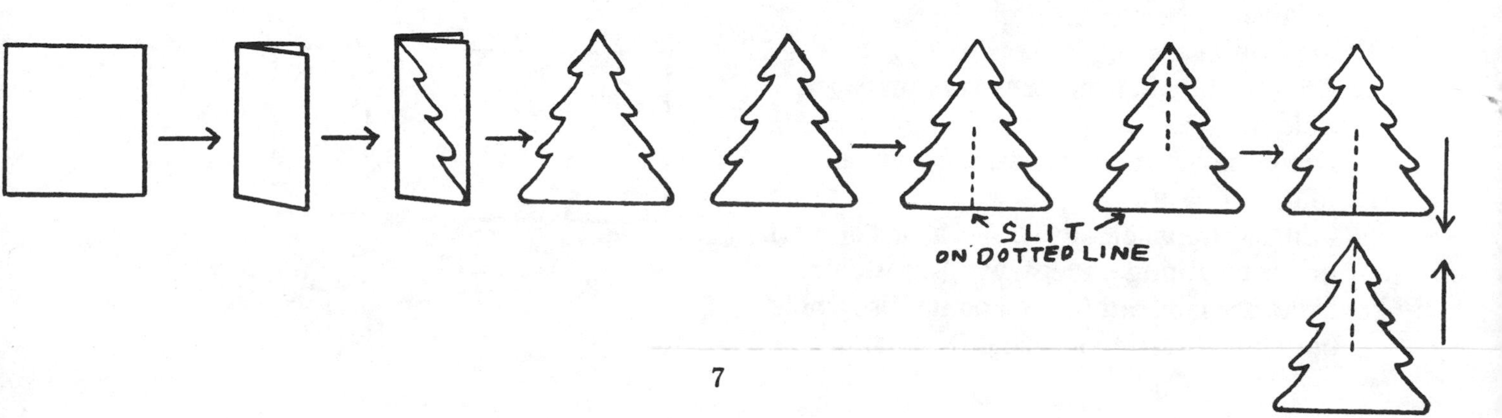

# All Creatures Great and Small: Stand-Up Animals

## Bible Story

**God Creates Animals (Genesis 1)**

Make different animals to show the wide variety of creatures God has placed in this world. Let these stand-ups remind you to thank God for all the different animals.

## Materials

Construction paper
Scissors
Glue
Markers or crayons (*optional*)
Pencil
Hole punch
Yarn

## Directions

**Tube animals**

1. Cut a rectangle from construction paper. Roll it and glue the ends to form a tube body.
2. Cut body parts such as legs, wings, ears, and a head from construction paper. You can cut identical pieces by folding the paper the needed number of times and cutting out several shapes at once.
3. Glue the pieces to the tube body. If needed, cut a slit in the tube body to insert the head or tail.
4. Use markers or crayons to add additional details.

**Folded animals**

1. Cut a rectangle from construction paper. Fold it.
2. Draw the outline of an animal along the fold. Cut it out.
3. Add additional details with crayons or markers or by gluing on legs, wings, ears, etc. Make the land animals stand up. Use a hole punch and yarn to suspend flying animals.

## Other Ideas

1. Use wallpaper or poster board to make the animals.
2. Add details with yarn, fabric, or crumpled tissue paper.
3. Have each child make several different animals to put on a box lid or Styrofoam tray.
4. Make a stand-up figure of Adam to name the animals.
5. Have the children make stand-up figures to illustrate one part of God's creation.

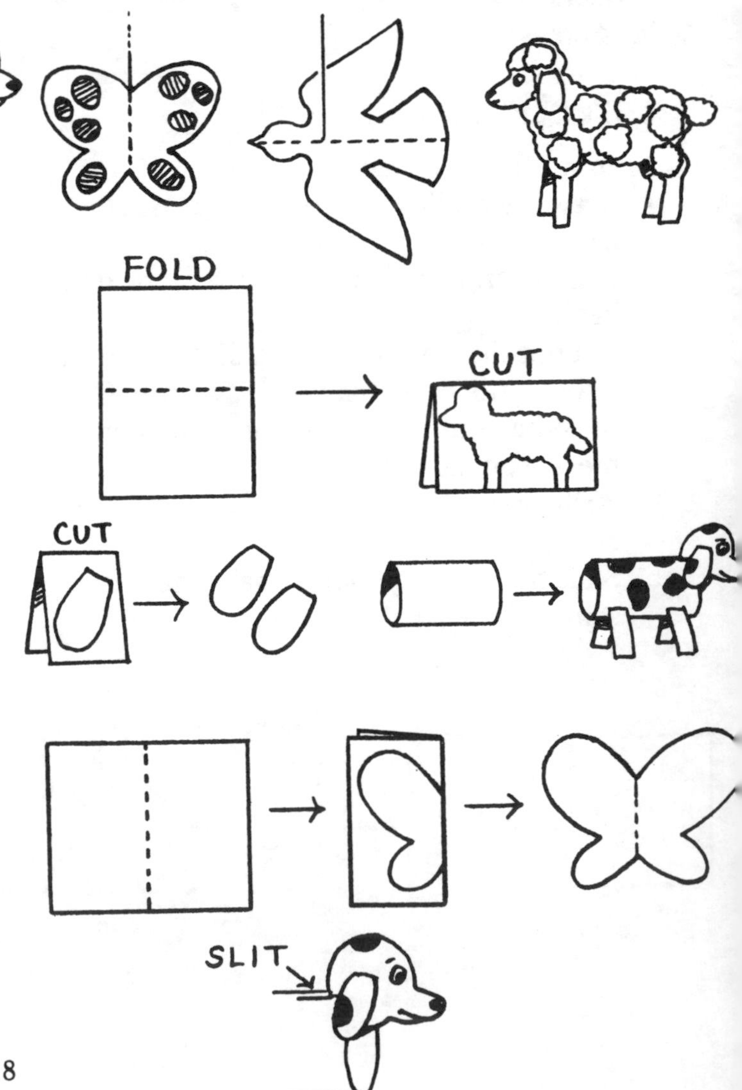

# God Made Me:
# Stand-Up Figures

## Bible Story

### Creation of Adam and Eve (Genesis 1:26–28; 2:7, 18–23)

God made Adam and Eve, and He made you. Make a stand-up self-portrait to celebrate God's beautiful creation.

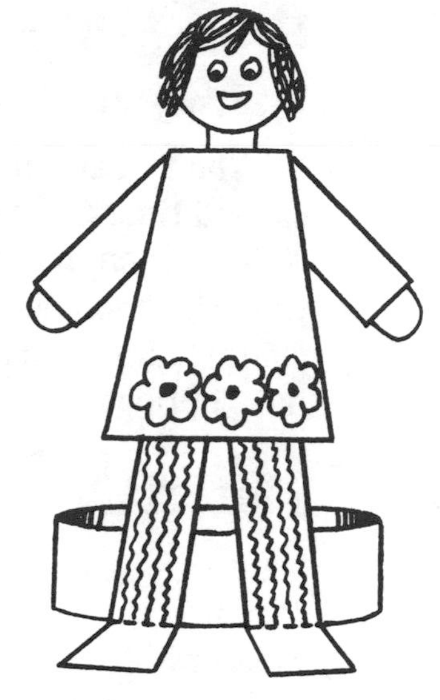

## Materials

Construction paper
Pencil
Scissors
Glue
Poster board

## Directions

1. Lightly sketch shapes on construction paper to make your self-portrait. Cut them out.
2. Glue the shapes together. Cut additional shapes for facial features and other details. Glue them on the body.
3. Cut a strip from poster board about ⅓ the height and twice the width of your figure. Write "God made (*your name*)" on one side of it.
4. Roll the strip and glue the ends together for a stand. Glue the bottom of your self-portrait to the stand.

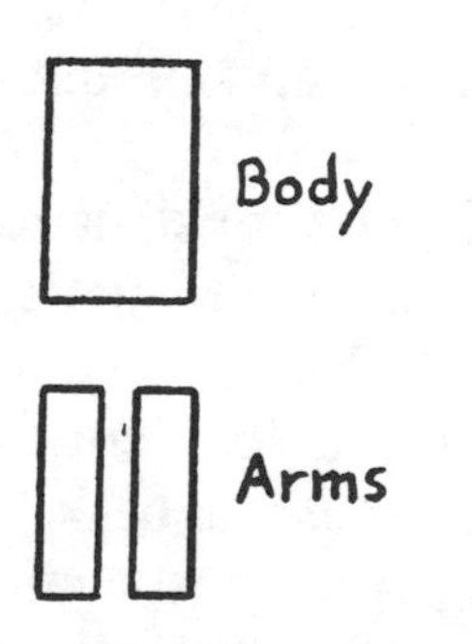


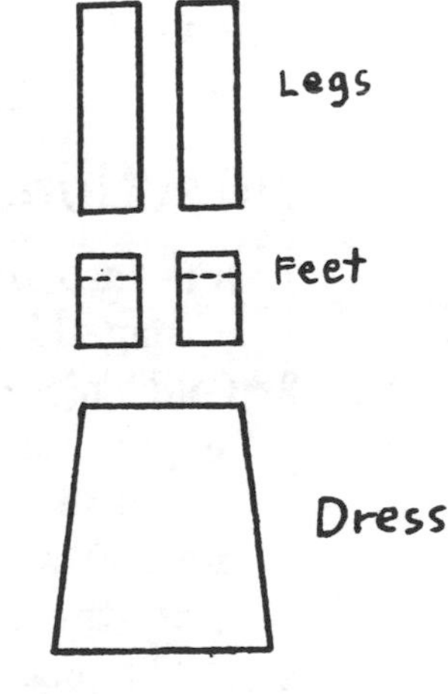


God Made

Hands

## Other Ideas

1. Glue shapes to a piece of construction paper.
2. Use markers to add details.
3. Cut shapes for clothes from wallpaper or wrapping paper.
4. Glue pieces of yarn and fabric on the body for details.
5. Use your class' stand-up figures with the story of Jesus and the children.
6. Make a cut-paper picture of your face.
7. Dress shapes in clothing from Bible times. Use them as puppets or figures in a diorama.
8. Cut shapes for a full-size self-portrait.
9. Show your figure doing something you like to do.

# 5 A Dove of Hope: Curled-Paper Bird

## Bible Story

**The Great Flood (Genesis 6:1–9:17)**

When Noah sent a dove out of the ark the second time, it flew over the flood and came back with an olive branch—a sign that the water had gone down and plants were growing again. Make a curled-paper sculpture of this dove of hope.

## Materials

White and green construction paper
Pencil
Scissors
Crayons or markers
Glue
Hole punch
Yarn

## Directions

1. If needed, duplicate and cut out the patterns on page 11.
2. Fold a piece of white construction paper lengthwise. Place the dove pattern on the fold as indicated. Trace and cut out the dove. Make sure you don't cut on the fold!
3. Color the dove's eyes and beak.
4. Fold a piece of green construction paper. Place the olive branch pattern on the fold as indicated. Trace and cut out the olive branch. Glue it in the dove's beak.
5. Cut narrow strips of white construction paper. To curl the strips, draw them across the full edge of a scissors.
6. Glue the curled strips on the wings of the dove for feathers.
7. Punch a hole in the top center of the dove. Cut a piece of yarn. Tie it through the hole for a hanger.

## Other Ideas

1. Omit the olive branch and use the dove for a symbol of the Holy Spirit.
2. Make different-colored birds to illustrate other Bible stories.

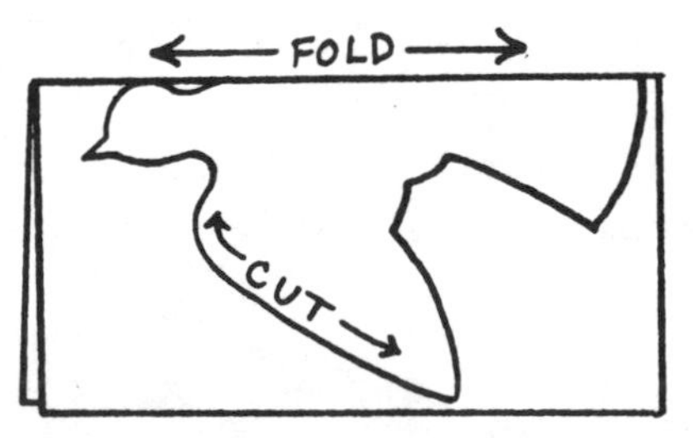


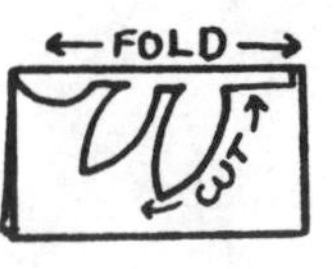

# Patterns for "A Dove of Hope"

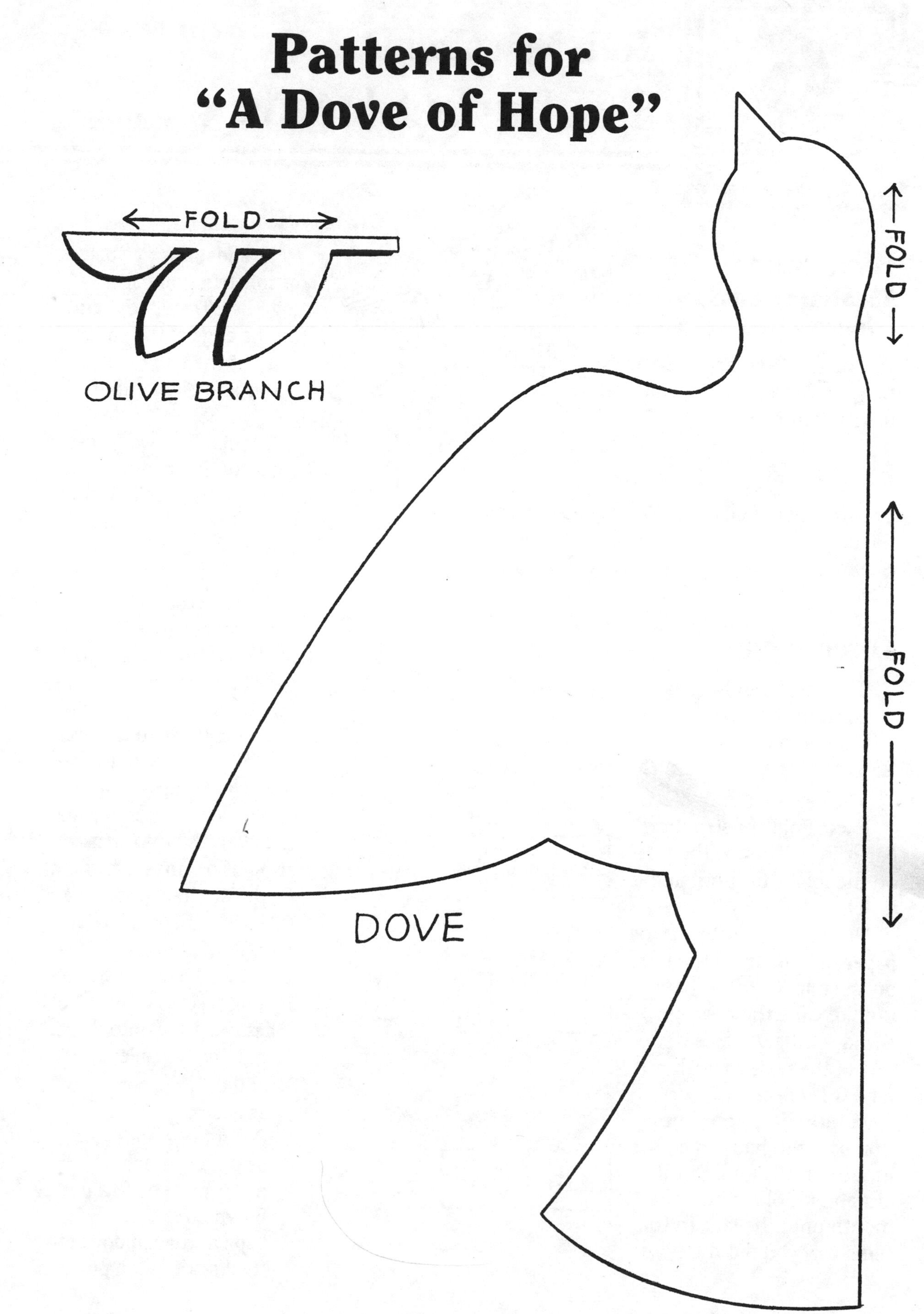

# To a New Land: 3-D Puppet Heads

## Bible Story

### Abraham and Sarah (Genesis 12:1–21:5)

God led Abraham and Sarah to a new land. Make 3-D puppets to tell their story.

## Materials

Construction paper
Pencil
Scissors
Glue
Paper plates or poster board (*optional*)
Wooden dowels

## Directions

1. If needed, duplicate and cut out the patterns on page 13. Modify features for each puppet.
2. Follow these directions to make each puppet head.

**Face:** Fold construction paper in half. Trace the face on the fold. Cut it out and unfold.

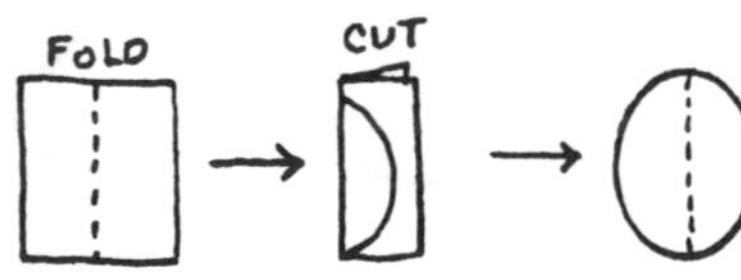


**Nose:** Fold construction paper in half. Trace the nose on the fold. Cut it out and unfold. Glue the nose onto the face. Allow the center fold of the nose to push out for a 3-D effect.

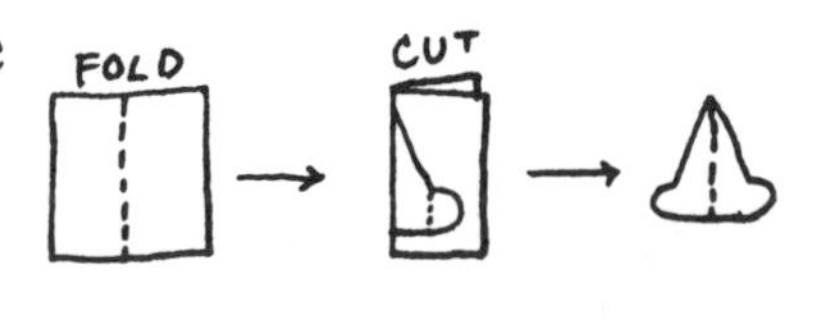


**Mouth:** Fold construction paper in half. Trace the mouth on the fold. Cut it out and unfold. Glue the mouth onto the face in the same way you did the nose.

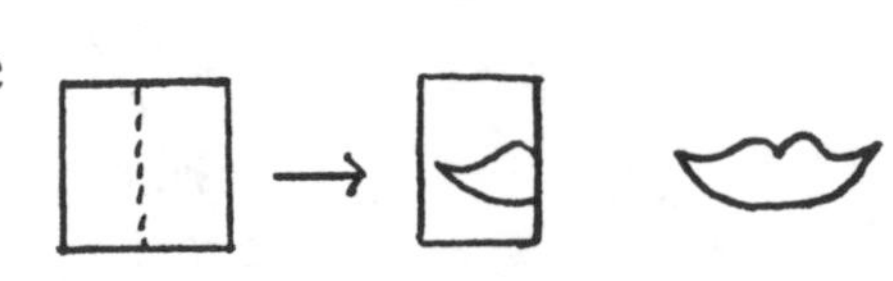

**Eyelids:** Put two pieces of construction paper together. Trace the eyelid on the edge of the paper. Cut out the half circles. Curve and glue onto the face.

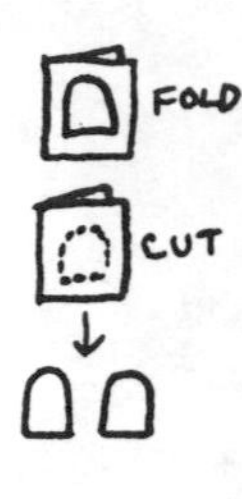


**Pupils:** Put two pieces of construction paper together. Trace the pupil on the paper. Cut out the circles. Glue them under the eyelids.

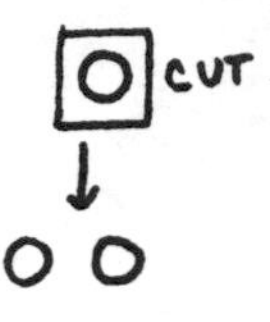


**Eyelashes:** Put two pieces of construction paper together. Cut two narrow rectangles the length of the eyelid. Fringe and glue these to the eyelid.

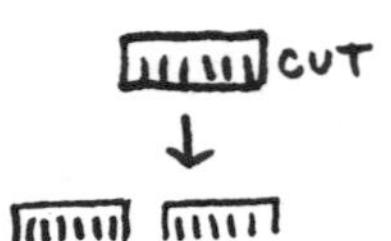


**Hair and Beard:** To create individual strips of hair put several long pieces of paper together. Cut into strips, straight or curved, for hair. Curl, if desired, or score and fold. Glue them onto the face. Trim as needed. To create fringed hair, cut fringes in long pieces of paper. Curl if desired. Glue onto the face. Trim as needed.

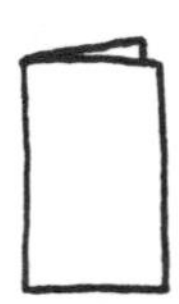

3. Add other paper features as desired.
4. For more stability, staple or glue the face to a paper plate or to a poster board circle.
5. Tape a wooden dowel to the back of each puppet.

# Patterns for "To a New Land"

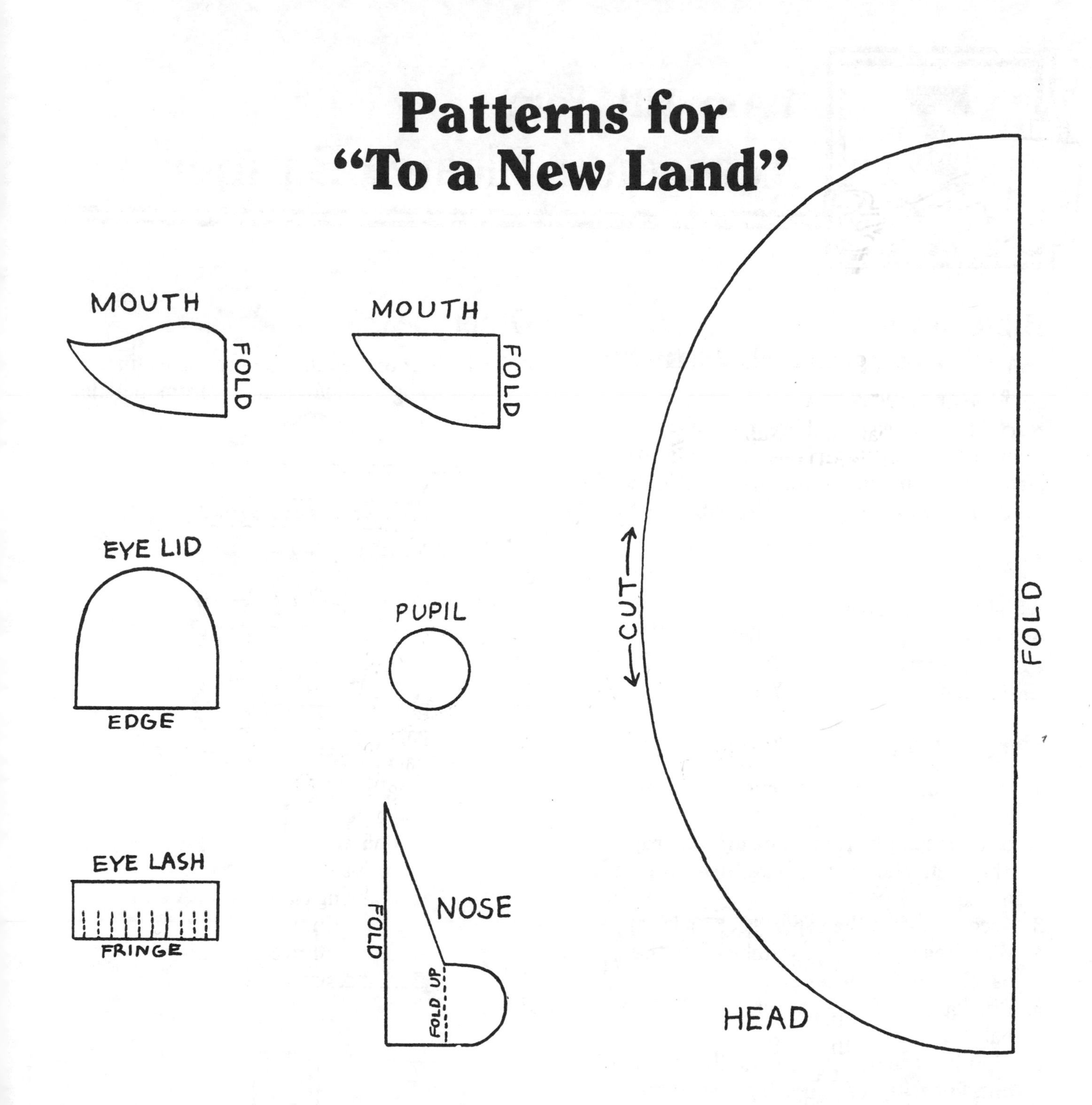


## Other Ideas

1. Make a smaller puppet for Isaac.
2. Make the puppets into masks. Omit the circle backing and cut holes in the puppets for eyes. To tie the mask on, attach yarn to each side. Or use the wooden dowel to hold the mask up to your face.
3. Make puppet heads for other Bible characters. Add paper details for crowns, turbans, and other features.
4. Cut out small puppets and tape them to drinking straws or craft sticks.
5. For a sturdier puppet, make the face from poster board.
6. Make hair from yarn, tissue paper, or crepe paper.
7. Trace a plate to make a circle head.

# 7 I Am with You: Accordion-Pleated Banner

## Bible Story

### Jacob's Dream (Genesis 28:10–22)

Jacob dreamed he saw a stairway that reached up to heaven. Above it stood the Lord, reminding Jacob of the Lord's promises to him. Make a paper banner to remind you that the Lord who was with Jacob is also with you.

## Materials

| | |
|---|---|
| White drawing paper | Pencil |
| Scissors | Glue |
| Drinking straw | Tape |
| Glitter pen | Yarn |

## Directions

1. If needed, duplicate and cut out the pattern on this page.
2. Cut a rectangle from white drawing paper. The width should be 1″ less than the length of the straw.
3. Accordion-fold the paper (back and forth).
4. Write the words "I am with you" on the paper with the glitter pen.
5. Cut squares of white paper. Fold them in half.
6. Lightly trace the angel along the fold. Cut it out. Put several squares together to cut multiple angels.
7. Unfold the angels and glue them to the stairway. Allow the center fold to push up for a 3-D effect.
8. Fold the top of the accordion-folded paper over the straw. Tape it in place. Cut a piece of yarn. Tie it to each end of the straw to make a hanger.

## Other Ideas

1. Add glitter or metallic stars to the banner.
2. Cut the angels and/or stairway from metallic paper.

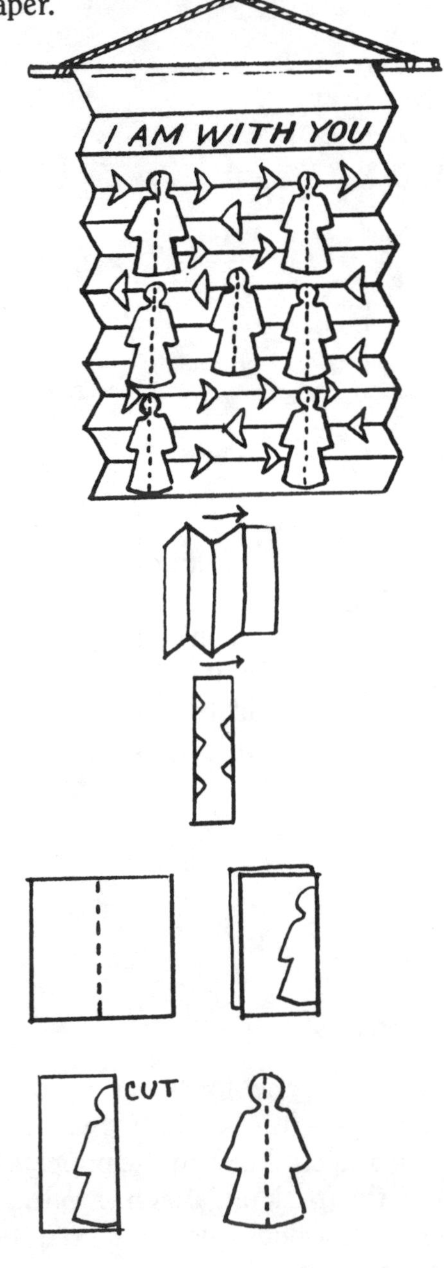

# A New Robe for Joseph: Torn-Paper Puppet

## Bible Story

### Jacob Gives Joseph a New Robe (Genesis 37:2–4)

What happened to Joseph after Jacob gave him a beautiful new robe? Make a torn-paper puppet to help you tell the story.

## Materials

Construction paper
Pencil
Scissors
Markers
Glue
Craft stick
Tape

## Directions

1. If needed, duplicate and cut out the patterns on this page.
2. Trace the outline of Joseph's robe on a piece of construction paper. Cut it out. Cut additional pieces for Joseph's head, hands, and feet.
3. Use markers to draw Joseph's eyes, nose, and mouth.
4. Glue on Joseph's head.
5. Tear construction-paper strips and glue them on to make Joseph's hair and robe. Trim the edges.
6. Glue on Joseph's hands and feet.
7. Tape Joseph to a craft stick.

## Other Ideas

1. Make a puppet to use as you tell about Joseph in Egypt.
2. Cut strips of paper instead of tearing them.
3. Cut a robe from wallpaper or wrapping paper.

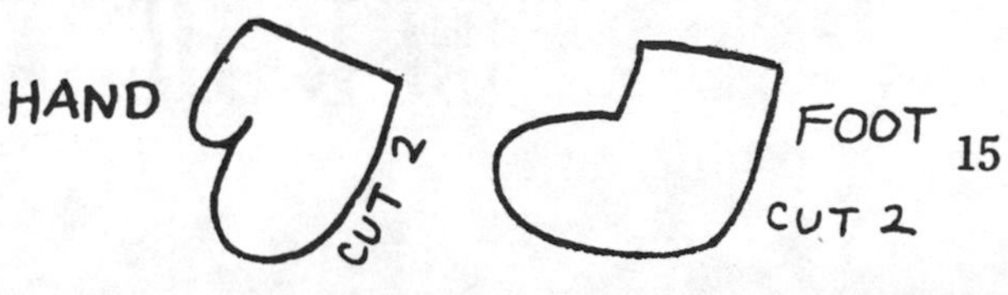


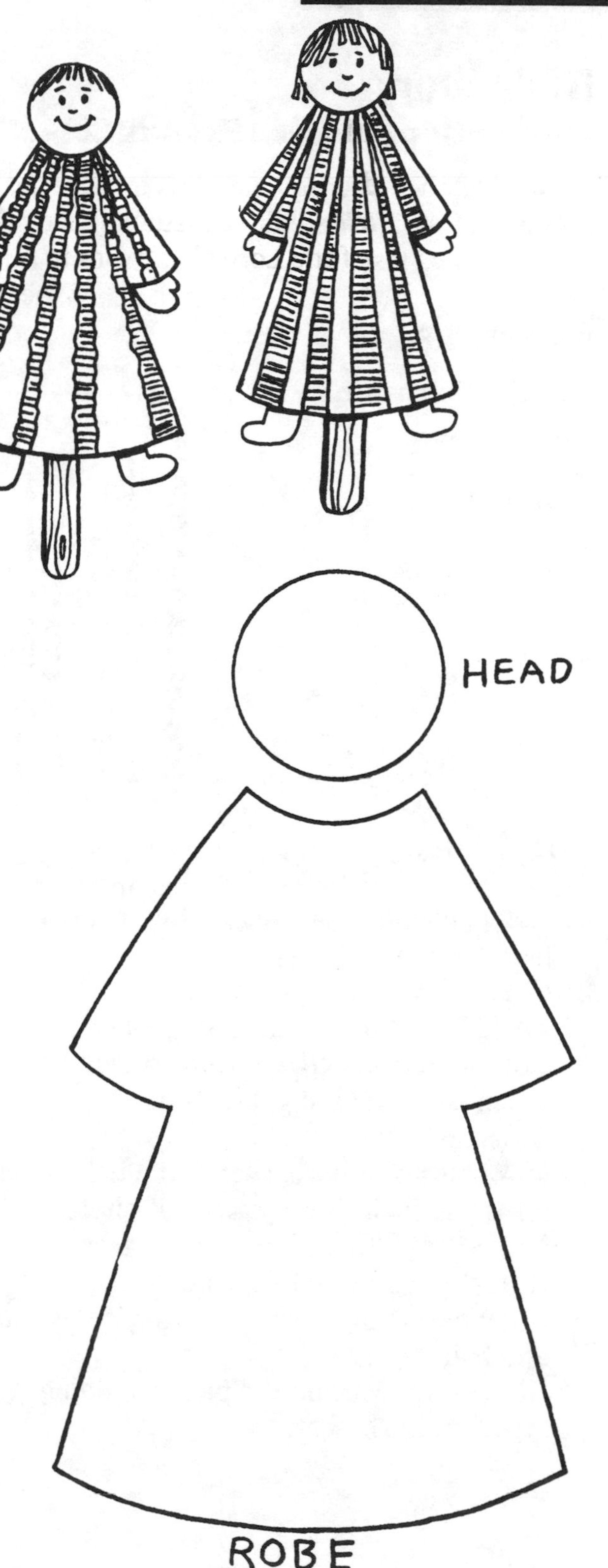

# 9 A Bed for Baby Moses: Shape Collage

## Bible Story

**The Birth of Moses (Exodus 2:1–10)**

God watched over Moses as his mother hid him from Pharaoh's soldiers. Make a shape collage to show Moses safe in his basket-bed.

## Materials

Construction paper
Scissors
Glue
Markers or crayons

## Other Ideas

1. Cut strips of paper for reeds.
2. Frame the picture by gluing it to a larger piece of construction paper.
3. Cut out shapes and glue them on for Miriam and Pharaoh's daughter.
4. Cut Moses' face and hair from construction paper.

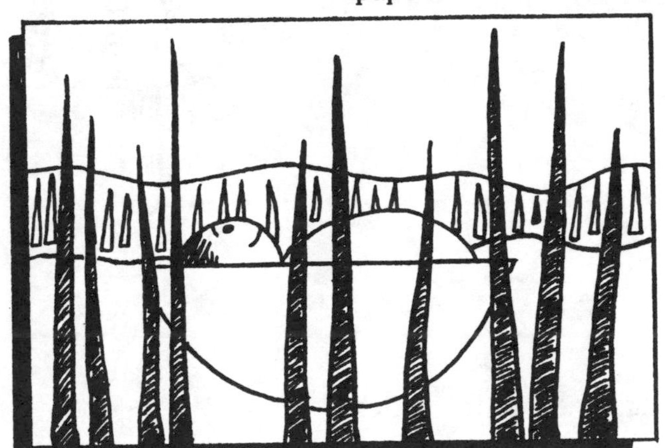

## Directions

1. Use a blue piece of construction paper for a background.
2. Cut a strip of yellow construction paper for sand. Glue it across the background.
3. Cut different lengths of thin triangles from green construction paper for reeds.
4. Glue a row of reeds along the sand.
5. Make Moses in his basket. Cut a half-circle for the basket. Cut a small half-circle for Moses' head. Cut a half-oval for Moses' body. Glue the shapes onto the paper.
6. Use markers or crayons to draw Moses' face and hair.
7. Glue more reeds on the picture, hiding Moses in his basket.

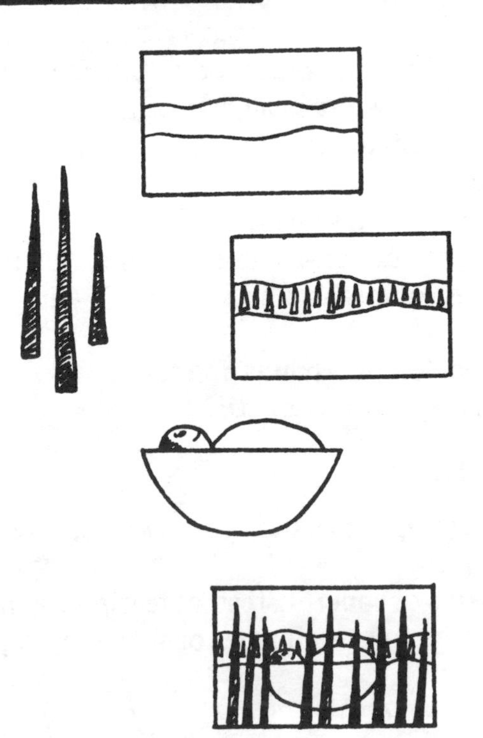

# Praise the Lord:
# Paper Weaving

## Bible Story

**The Songs of Moses and Miriam (Exodus 15:1–21)**

Moses and Miriam sang songs of praise to God for leading His people safely through the waters of the Red Sea. Weave a praise picture to remind you to praise the Lord for the ways He helps you.

PRAISE THE LORD

## Materials

Construction paper
Scissors
Glue
Markers or crayons

## Directions

1. Use a piece of blue construction paper for a background.
2. Fold the blue paper in half. Cut several rows of wavy lines across the paper to represent the Red Sea. Stop cutting 1″ from the edge of the paper. Unfold the sheet.
3. Cut strips of different-colored construction paper.
4. Weave the strips through the wavy lines, alternating the lines. Glue the ends of the strips. Trim if necessary.
5. Write "Praise the Lord" on the bottom of the paper.

## Other Ideas

1. Write the words sung by Moses or Miriam from Exodus 15 onto your praise picture.
2. Weave ribbon or strips of metallic paper or tissue paper into the background paper.
3. Cut the strips to be woven in wavy lines, numbering each strip as you cut it. Then weave the strips in the same order in which they were cut. (When weaving wavy strips, it is important that they all fit together in order.) You could also cut a pattern and trace strips in different colors.
4. Use this project for any lesson that emphasizes praise and thanksgiving.
5. Weave colorful place mats. Laminate them and use when your class enjoys snacks.

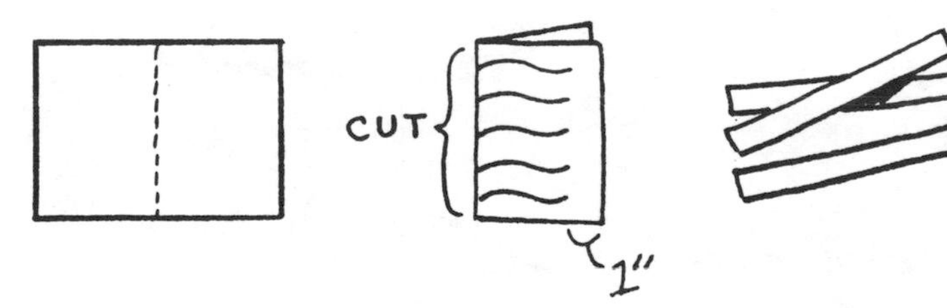


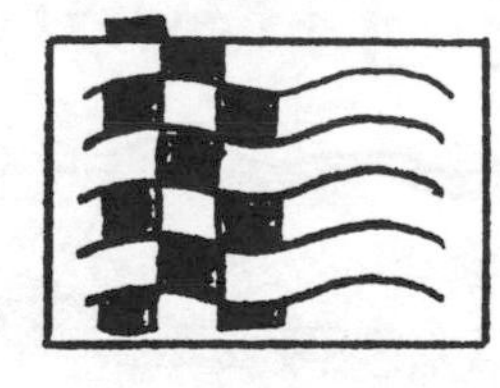

# O Give Thanks: Papier-Mâché Fruit Bowl

## Bible Story

**God Sends Manna and Quail to Feed His People (Exodus 16)**

God provided manna and quail to feed His people in the wilderness. He also gives us the food we need each day. Make a papier-mâché fruit bowl to show some of the good fruits God gives to us.

## Materials

Two bowls
Flour
Water
Spoon
Old vinyl tablecloth
Newspaper
Scissors
Tempera paint
Paintbrush

## Directions

1. Make flour paste: In a bowl combine ½ cup flour with ⅔ cup water. Stir until creamy. Thicken the paste with flour or thin it with water as desired. (Makes ½ pint.)
2. Cover your work area with an old vinyl tablecloth.
3. **Bowl**
   a. Cut four to six newspaper squares a little larger than the outside of the bowl you will use for a mold.
   b. Place the bowl you are using for a mold upside down in front of you.
   c. Place one piece of newspaper over the bowl. Spread paste over the paper.
   d. Dip a second piece of newspaper into the paste. Place it over the first piece. Spread the paste evenly over it. Continue until the desired number of newspaper pieces are used.
   e. Set the bowl aside to dry. (Drying should take one or two days, depending on the thickness of the wet newspaper.)
   f. Paint the bowl with tempera paint. When dry, paint the words "O Give Thanks" on the bowl.

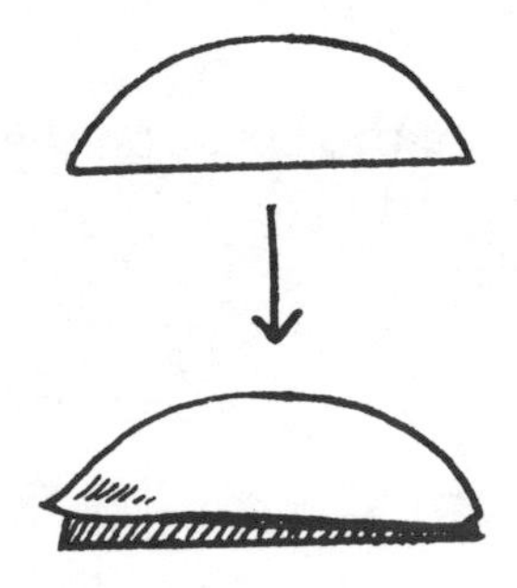

4. **Fruit**
   a. Tear newspaper into half pages and into strips of varying thicknesses and lengths.
   b. Crumple and shape newspaper to represent different kinds of fruit.
   c. Dip newspaper strips into the paste and wrap them around the crumpled shapes. Wrap several layers, using thinner strips for a smoother finish.
   d. Let the fruit dry several days, turning it occasionally.
   e. Paint the fruit with tempera paint.
   f. Place the fruit in the bowl.

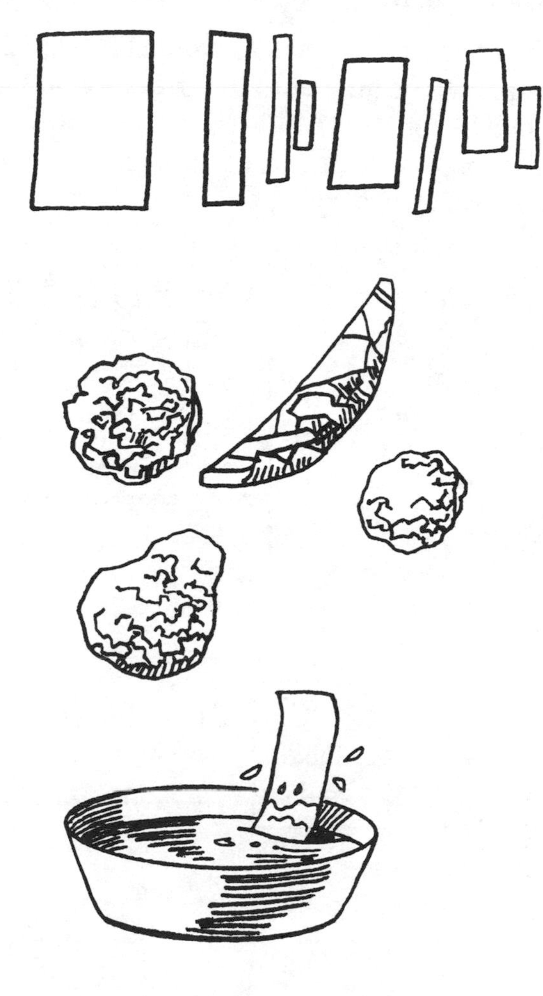

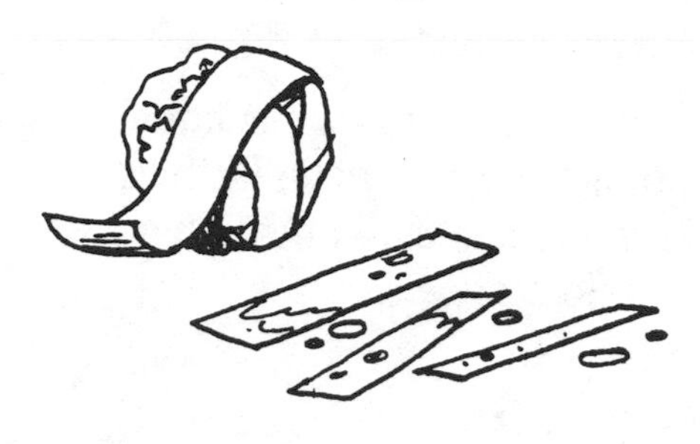

## Other Ideas

1. Spray or paint the bowl and fruit with acrylic varnish.
2. Use the bowl and fruit with other Bible stories about God's gift of food.
3. Weave a basket from paper strips.
4. Make other kinds of food from papier mâché.

# David and His Sheep: Bag Puppets

## Bible Story

**David the Shepherd**
**(1 Samuel 16:11; 17:33–37)**

David once cared for his father's sheep. Make bag puppets to help you tell the story of how David took good care of the sheep in his father's flock.

## Materials

Paper bag (lunch size)
Construction paper
Pencil
Scissors
Glue
Markers or crayons

## Directions

1. Use the bottom of the bag as a pattern to trace a white rectangle for each sheep and a flesh-colored rectangle for David. Cut them out. These will be the face pieces.
2. Cut a strip of the same color, about 1½″ wide, to go below the bottom flap of each bag. These will be the lower jaws of the puppets.
3. Glue the rectangle faces and strips of paper onto the bottom of the bags.
4. Use markers to draw eyes and a nose on the rectangles for David and the sheep. Draw the bottom of their mouths on the paper strips.
5. Cut and glue on ears for the sheep.
6. Cut brown paper into narrow strips. Curl each strip over the edge of a dull scissors. Glue these on the David puppet for hair.
7. Curl white paper strips into loops. Glue them on the sheep puppets for wool.

## Other Ideas

1. Use the sheep puppets as you read Psalm 23.
2. Make a Jesus puppet to tell the story of the Good Shepherd.
3. Instead of using markers, cut facial features from construction paper.

# A Circle of Friends: Series Cutting

## Bible Story

**David and Jonathan (1 Samuel 18:1–4)**

God gave David and Jonathan a special friendship. Who are your friends? Cut a "circle of friends" to help you remember to thank God for His gift of friends.

## Materials

Two colors of construction paper
Scissors
Pencil
Glue
Fine-tipped markers

## Directions

1. Using different colors of construction paper, cut two circles. Fold one circle in half. Fold the same circle a second time.
2. Using the pattern, trace half of a child on each fold. Connect their arms. Draw half a heart inside each child's body.
3. Cut out the shapes. Be careful not to cut along the folds!
4. Unfold the circle. Glue it to the other construction paper circle. Glue the cut-out hearts between the figures.
5. Write "Thank You, God, for my friends" around the circle.

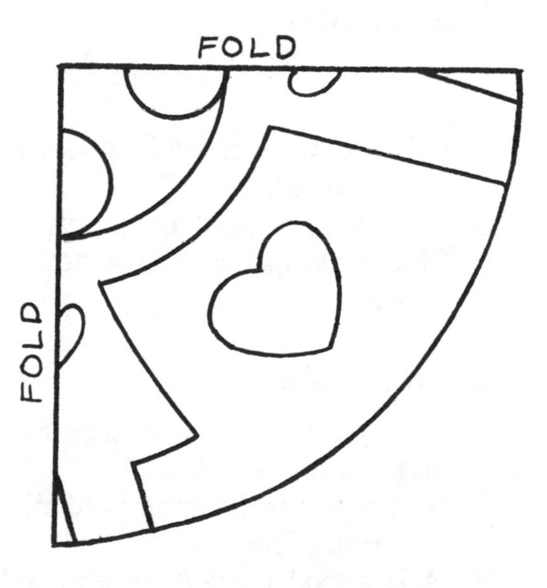


## Other Ideas

1. Fold paper into sixths or eighths, depending on the size of the circle and the detail of the pattern. Cut different designs into different folds.
2. Only cut hearts into the folded paper.
3. Glue the series cutting to tissue paper. Hang the circle in a window as a sun catcher.
4. Use this project with the stories of David and Mephibosheth, the Good Samaritan, or Jesus and the children.
5. Write "Love One Another" or a similar verse on the circle.

# A House for the Lord: Paper-Strip Construction

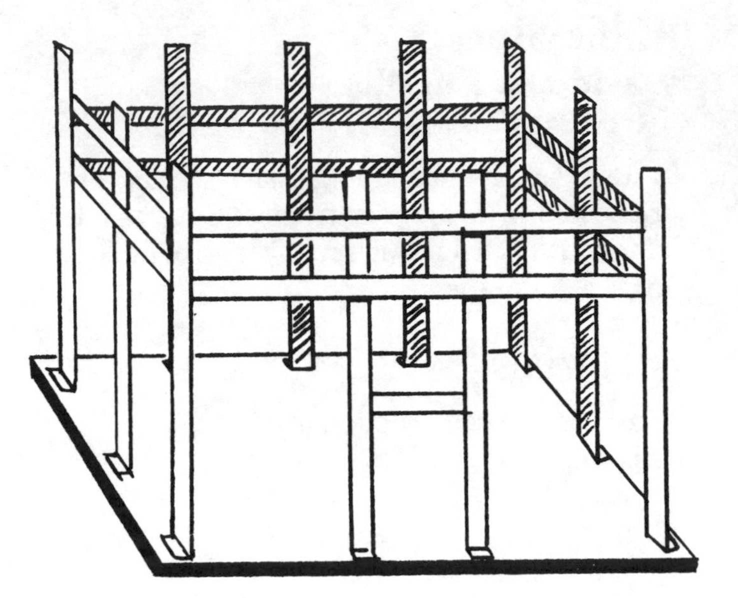

## Bible Story

**Solomon Builds the Temple (1 Kings 6)**

Solomon built the temple for the Lord. What do you think it looked like? Use paper strips to build a model temple.

## Materials

Construction paper
Ruler
Pencil
Scissors
Glue

## Directions

1. Measure and cut construction paper into 1″ strips.
2. Fold the strips in half lengthwise to make posts and pillars.
3. Use a piece of construction paper for a base. Glue the strips together to build your model temple.

## Other Ideas

1. Build your temple on a piece of cardboard or Styrofoam.
2. Glue together different-sized pieces of construction paper.
3. Make a model of your church or design a new church building.
4. Cut strips from poster board for more stability.

# Young King Joash: Paper Crown

## Bible Story

**Young Joash Is Crowned King of Judah (2 Chronicles 24)**

Joash was seven years old when he became king. The Bible says that for many years he did what was right in the sight of the Lord. Make a crown to wear as you tell the story of the life of Joash.

## Materials

Construction paper
Scissors
Tape
Glue

## Directions

1. Accordion-fold a strip of paper long enough to fit around your head. Cut a crown design into it. Unfold it. If desired, curl the crown points outward.
2. Fit the crown to your head. Tape the ends together.
3. Using different colors of construction paper, cut several strips ½″ wide.
   a. **Make coil jewels:** Roll or curl a strip of paper. Glue the outside end. Glue the jewels on the crown.
   b. **Decorative lines:** Curl or fold paper strips. Glue them flat to the crown. Use tape if necessary.

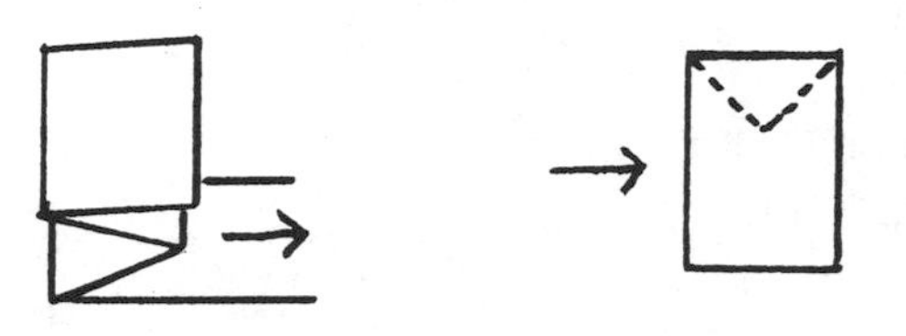

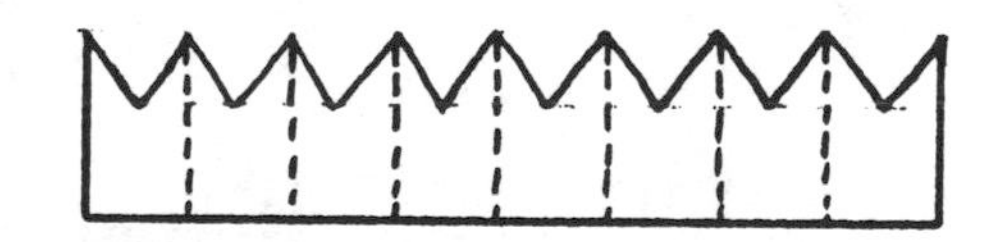

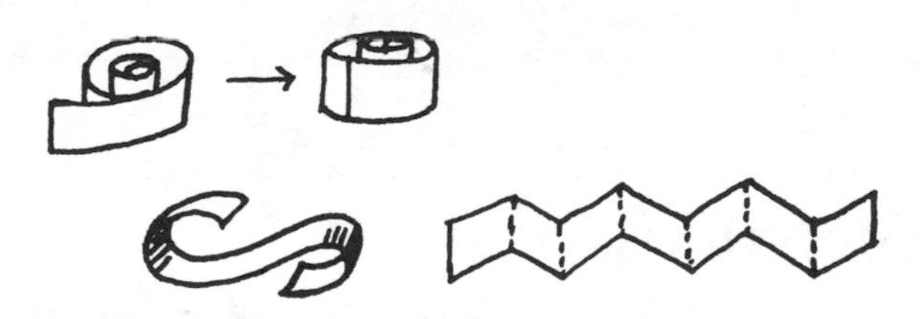

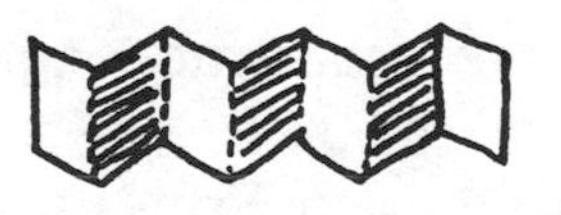

## Other Ideas

1. Fold crown points out for a 3-D effect.
2. Make a "crown of life" for use with lessons about heaven.
3. Glue pieces of crushed or flat tissue paper onto the crown.
4. Use metallic wrapping paper to make the crown and jewels.
5. Use this project with Bible stories about kings or queens.
6. Write "The Lord Is My King" or another reference about the kingship of God on the crown.

# Three Days in a Fish: Action-Figure Puppets

## Bible Story

**Jonah and the Great Fish (Jonah 1–2)**

What was Jonah doing in the stomach of a big fish? Make action-figure puppets to help you tell how God took care of Jonah.

## Materials

Construction paper
Pencil
Scissors
Glue
Markers or crayons
Paper fastener
Yarn
Tape

## Directions

1. Duplicate and cut out the patterns on page 25.
2. Trace the figures on construction paper. Cut them out.
3. Glue the fins on the fish. Fringe the fins and tail.
4. Use crayons or markers to color Jonah and add details.
5. Fasten the jaws onto the fish with the paper fastener.
6. Cut a 12″ piece of yarn. Tape one end of the yarn to Jonah and the other end to the mouth of the fish.

## Other Ideas

1. Cut the fish and fins as one piece. Add details with crayons or markers.
2. Attach the fish and Jonah shapes to craft sticks or wooden dowels and use as puppets.
3. Glue the shapes to a sheet of construction paper to make a picture. Push the paper fastener through the background paper to attach the fish's jaws.

# Pattern Pieces for "Three Days in a Fish"

# Brave Queen Esther: Tube Puppet

## Bible Story

**Queen Esther Saves Her People (Esther)**

It took a brave queen to stop a plot to kill her people. Make a tube puppet to help you tell the story of Esther's bravery.

## Materials

Construction paper
Scissors
Glue
Tissue paper
Drinking straw
Masking tape

## Directions

1. Duplicate and cut out the patterns on page 27.
2. Cut an 8¼" × 5½" rectangle from flesh-colored construction paper. Roll the rectangle into a tube. Glue the edge.
3. Cut strips of black paper for hair. Curl the strips by pulling them across the edge of a dull scissors. Glue the strips on the tube for hair. (If you use the pattern, fringe the bangs and cut strips into the hair.)
4. Cut a strip of yellow construction paper for a crown. Accordion-fold it and cut a triangle out of the top. Glue small pieces of colored tissue paper to the crown for jewels. Glue the crown around the top of the puppet.
5. Cut a nose, a mouth, and two eyes. Glue these to the face.
6. Tape a straw to the inside of the tube.

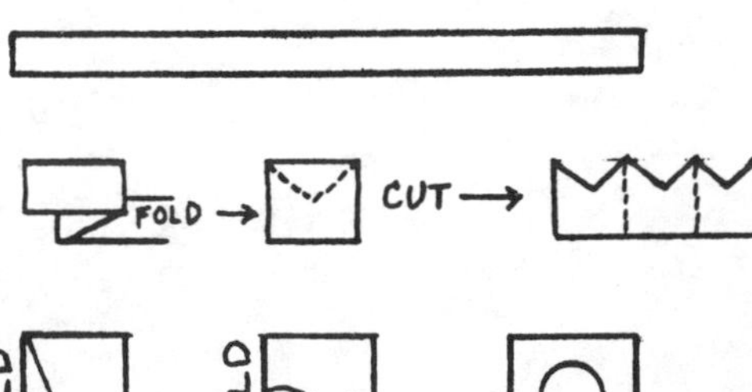

## Other Ideas

1. Use a craft stick instead of a drinking straw. Tape a wooden dowel to a larger puppet.
2. Add a strip of paper at the bottom of the tube for the top of a robe.
3. Draw facial features on the paper with a marker.
4. Put the crown on when Esther becomes queen.

# Pattern Pieces for "Brave Queen Esther"

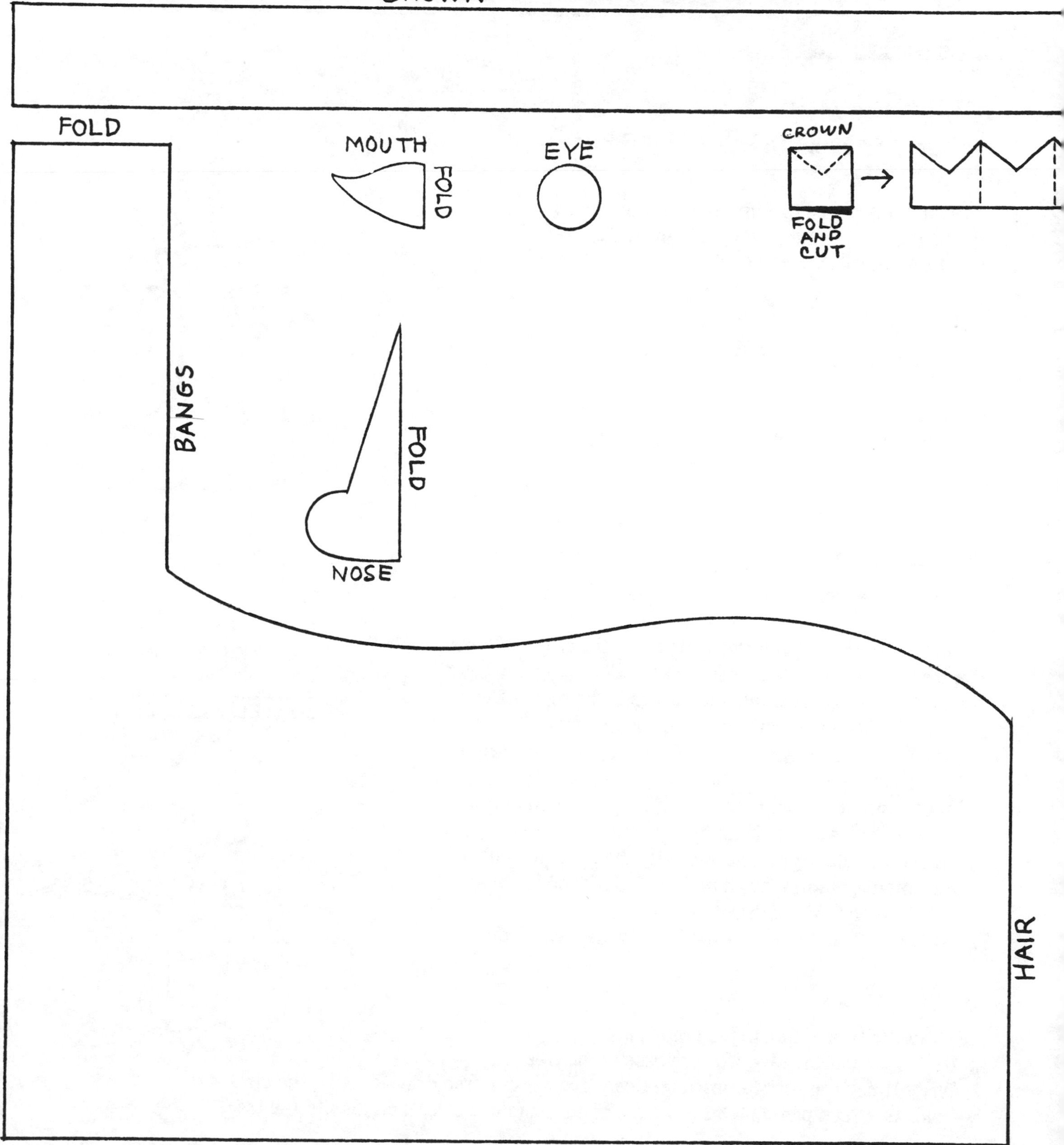

# Waiting for the Lord: Fringed Jesse Tree

## Bible Story

**Isaiah Writes of the Coming Savior (Isaiah 53)**

Make a Jesse tree to remind you of the many Old Testament people who waited for the coming of the promised Savior.

## Materials

Poster board
Scissors
Stapler
Green and yellow construction paper
Glue
Fine-tipped markers

## Directions

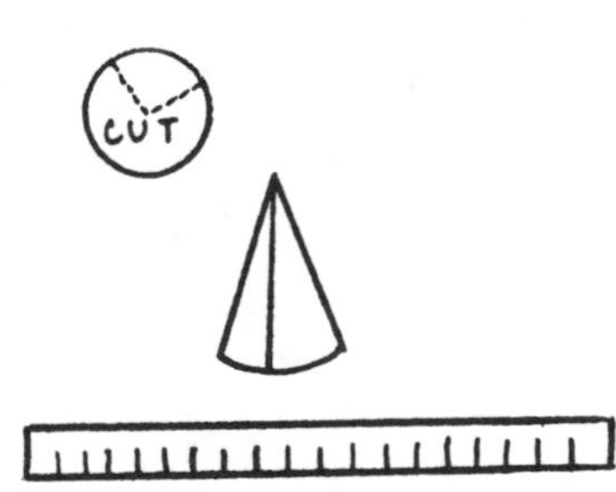


1. Cut a circle from poster board . Cut out ⅓ of the circle as a wedge.
2. Staple the sides of the remaining ⅔ of the circle to form a tree.
3. Cut strips of green construction paper. Fringe one edge.
4. Wrap the strips around the tree, starting from the bottom. Glue each strip in place. Continue until the whole tree is covered.

5. Trace a small circle on one piece of paper, then cut out several circles at one time.
6. On each circle ornament, write the name of an Old Testament person who waited for God's promise of a Savior to be fulfilled. Start with Isaiah.
7. Cut a star to go on top of the tree. Write "Jesus" on it.

## Other Ideas

1. Wrap the tree with fringed crepe paper.
2. Use construction paper for the base of the tree.
3. Write the names on gummed circles. Have the children draw faces on the circles.
4. Fold the green paper strips in half. Fringe the folded side, then glue to the tree.

# A Light for All People: Advent Card

## Bible Story

### The Birth of John (Luke 1:57–80)

Make an Advent card to help someone else get ready for Christmas, the time when Jesus, our light, came for all people.

## Materials

White drawing paper
Scissors
Pencil
Markers
Glue
Envelope (3⅝″ × 6½″)

## Directions

1. If needed, duplicate and cut out the pattern on this page.
2. Cut a strip of white paper about 5½″ wide and 10″ long.
3. Accordion-fold the paper (back and forth) into four equal parts.
4. Lay the pattern along the fold as indicated and trace the flame. Cut out the candles. Unfold them.
5. Use colorful markers to write these words in order, one on each candle: *Hope, Peace, Joy, Love.*
6. Draw a manger with Baby Jesus on the last candle.
7. Copy the instructions in the box. Glue them to the back of the first candle.
8. Sign your name. Put the card in an envelope and send it to someone during the first week of Advent.

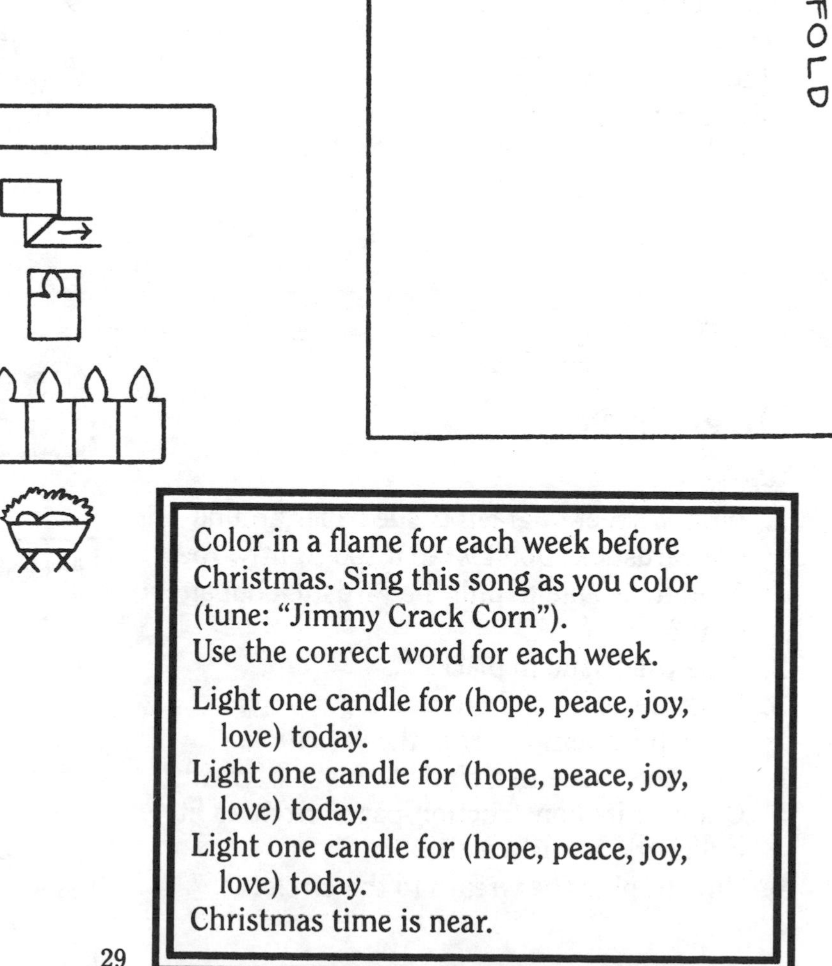


Color in a flame for each week before Christmas. Sing this song as you color (tune: “Jimmy Crack Corn”).
Use the correct word for each week.

Light one candle for (hope, peace, joy, love) today.
Light one candle for (hope, peace, joy, love) today.
Light one candle for (hope, peace, joy, love) today.
Christmas time is near.

# Countdown to Christmas: Wreath and Candle

## Bible Story

**An Angel Appears to Zechariah (Luke 1:5–25)**

John's birth began the countdown to the long-awaited birth of Jesus. Make a crushed-paper wreath and Christ candle to help mark the days that lead to Christmas.

## Materials

Green, red, and yellow tissue paper
Yardstick
Tape
White construction paper
Scissors
Glue
Glitter pen
Pencil

## Directions

**Wreath**

1. Wrap a sheet of green tissue paper around the yardstick. Don't wrap it too tightly. You need to be able to pull the yardstick out after step 3.
2. Tape the tissue in place.
3. Push the ends of the tissue together to crunch it. Remove from the yardstick.
4. Tape the tissue in a circle to make a wreath.
5. Cut a white construction-paper circle to fit under the tissue wreath.
6. Tape or glue the wreath to the circle.

**Candle**

1. Cut a rectangle from white construction paper the width of the inside of your circle.
2. The Greek letters *chi* (Χ) and *rho* (P) were used by early Christians as an abbreviation for *Christ.* Use a glitter pen to write ☧ in the middle of the rectangle.
3. Roll the rectangle into a tall tube and tape the edge.
4. Trace the circular end of the tube on a piece of white paper. Enlarge the circle ¼". Cut it out. Cut a ¼" hole in the center of the circle.
5. Cut tabs around the circle edge ¼" deep. Bend them down and fit the circle into the top end of the candle. Glue it in place.
6. Tape or glue the candle inside the tissue-paper ring.
7. Cut a rectangle from yellow tissue paper. Roll it together lengthwise. Pinch both ends. On Christmas Day, glue one end inside the hole in the center of the candle for a flame.

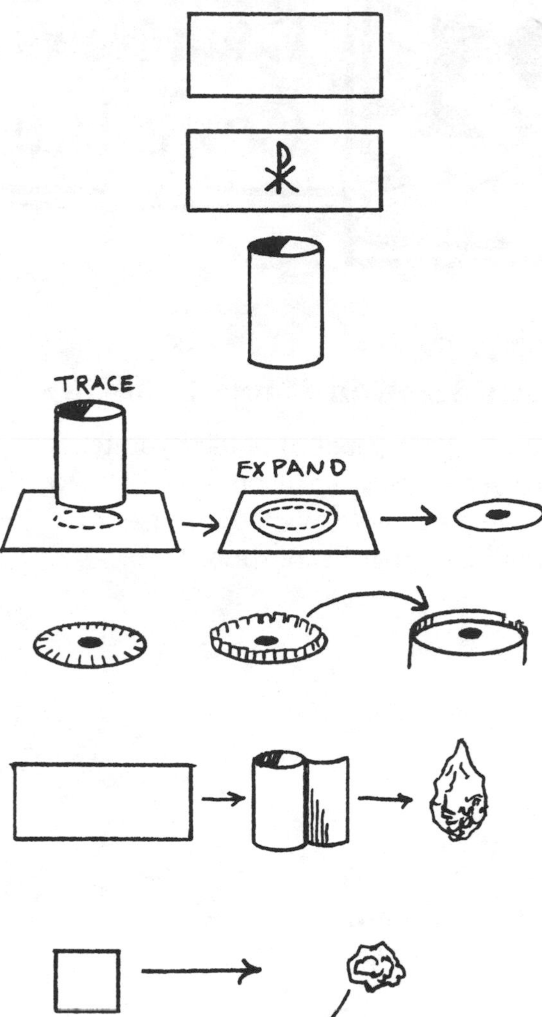


**Tissue Balls**

1. Cut a red tissue square (about ½") for each day in the four weeks before Christmas.
2. Each day, crumple one square and glue it to the wreath.

## Other Ideas

1. Write ☧ on the side of the candle with markers, crayons, or glitter and glue. Or cut the letters from construction paper or metallic paper.
2. Roll three pieces of purple (or blue) construction paper and one piece of pink into candles. Fit the four candles into holes cut into a Styrofoam wreath. Glue a tissue flame to the top of one of the candles for each of the four weeks in Advent.
3. Wrap the wreath with ribbon or metallic star garland.
4. Cut the candle flame from metallic paper.
5. Glue on metallic sequins for each day of Advent.
6. Use red gummed labels instead of red tissue paper.
7. Omit the candle in the center of the wreath. Add a bow made from tissue paper or ribbon to the wreath. On the paper in the center of the wreath write the words "Come, Lord Jesus" for Advent or "Christ, the Savior, Is Born" for Christmas. Punch a hole at the top of the paper backing. Tie a piece of yarn through it. Hang the wreath.
8. Place a real Christ candle in the center of the wreath. (*Do not light.*)

# Good News from Gabriel: Cone Puppet

## Bible Story

**The Annunciation (Luke 1:26–38)**

Make an angel puppet to hold as you tell how Gabriel told Mary she would be the mother of the long-awaited Savior. Then use the angel for a Christmas decoration.

## Materials

Wallpaper
Pencil
Scissors
Craft glue
Drinking straw
Styrofoam ball
Red and blue or brown construction paper
Hole punch
Spanish moss

## Directions

1. Duplicate and cut out the patterns on page 33.
2. Trace the large half circle onto a piece of wallpaper. Cut it out. Glue the edges together to make a cone.
3. Trace two quarter circles onto a piece of wallpaper. Cut them out. Glue the edges of each together to make arms. Glue one arm to each side of the cone.
4. Fold a piece of wallpaper in half. Trace the small half circle on the fold. Cut a small hole the middle of the half circle. Unfold the circle. Glue it over the top of the cone for a cape.
5. Fold a piece of wallpaper in half. Trace the wings on the fold. Cut out the wings. Unfold them and glue them on the back of the angel.
6. Cut 2″ from a drinking straw. Insert one end into the Styrofoam ball. Insert the other end into the hole at the top of the cone.
7. Punch out two circles from blue or brown construction paper. Glue them on the Styrofoam ball for eyes. Punch out one circle from red construction paper. Glue it on for a mouth.
8. Glue Spanish moss onto the Styrofoam ball for hair.

## Other Ideas

1. Cut the angel pattern pieces from white paper, decorative wrapping paper, or metallic paper.
2. Make a paper head for the angel.
3. Glue on the Styrofoam ball with a glue gun.
4. Use yellow Easter grass for hair.
5. Add paper doily sections, glitter, metallic garland, or sequins to the angel.

# Pattern Pieces for "Good News from Gabriel"

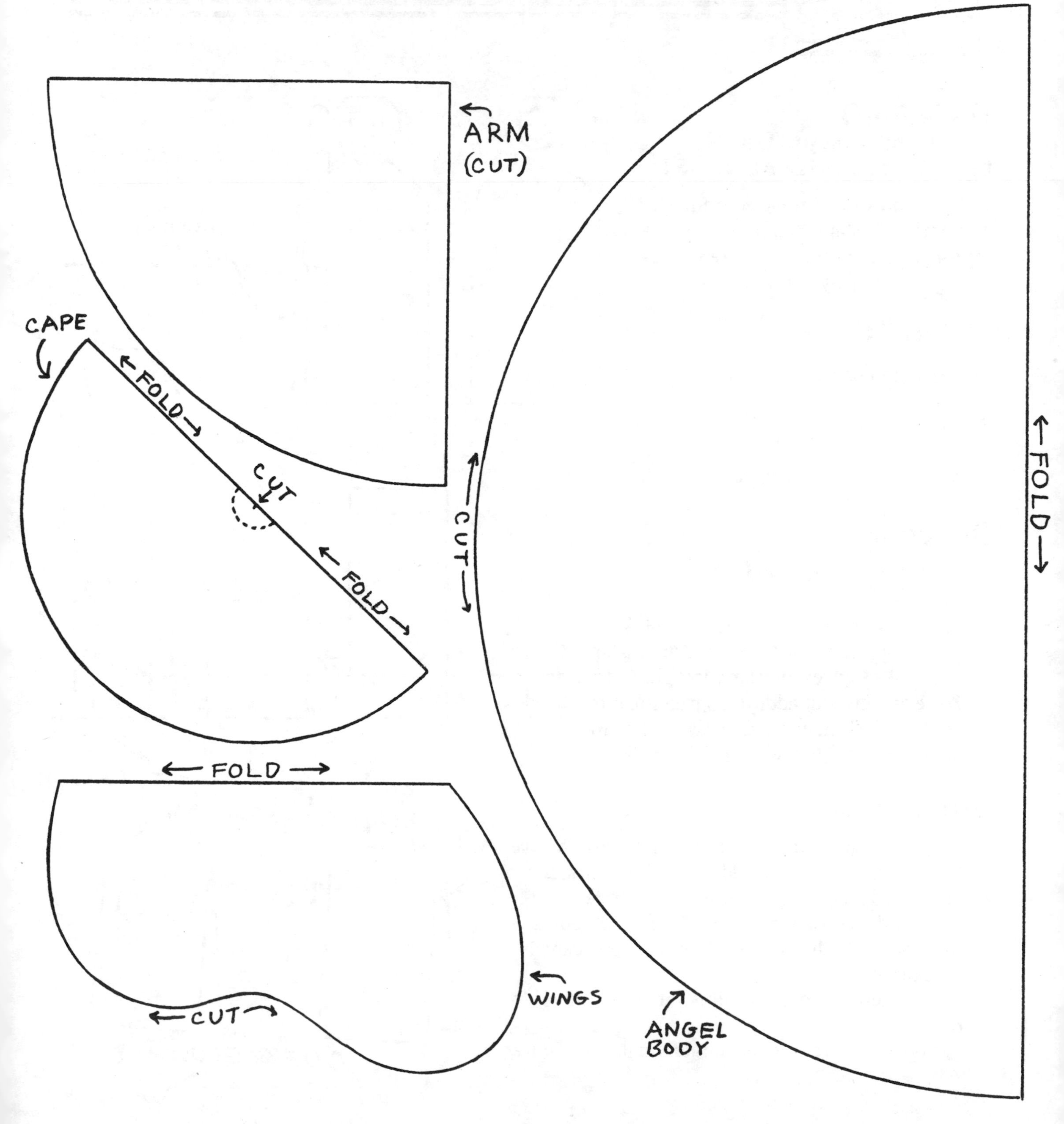

# 22 The Road to Bethlehem: Single-Fold Figures

## Bible Story

### Mary and Joseph Travel to Bethlehem (Luke 2:1–5)

Mary and Joseph traveled from Nazareth to distant Bethlehem to register for the emperor's tax. Make single-fold figures to play-act their journey.

## Materials

Construction paper
Pencil
Scissors
Glue
Markers or crayons (*optional*)

## Directions

1. If needed, duplicate and cut out the patterns on page 35.
2. Fold the construction paper in half. With the fold at the top, trace the figure you are making. Cut it out. Make figures for Mary, Joseph, and the donkey.
3. Trace and cut out additional paper features to add details. Glue them on. Or draw on features.
4. Stand up the figures for an Advent display.

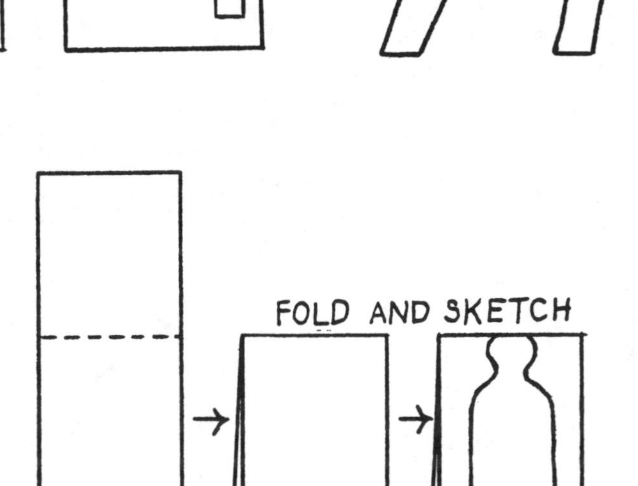


## Other Ideas

1. Place the figures under the tree on Christmas Eve. Make a baby Jesus and add it for a nativity scene.
2. Use folded shapes and figures to illustrate other parts of the Christmas story. Make a few figures each week of Advent. Make Wise Men and camels for Epiphany.
3. Use single-fold figures to illustrate other Bible stories.
4. Use poster board to make larger single-fold figures.

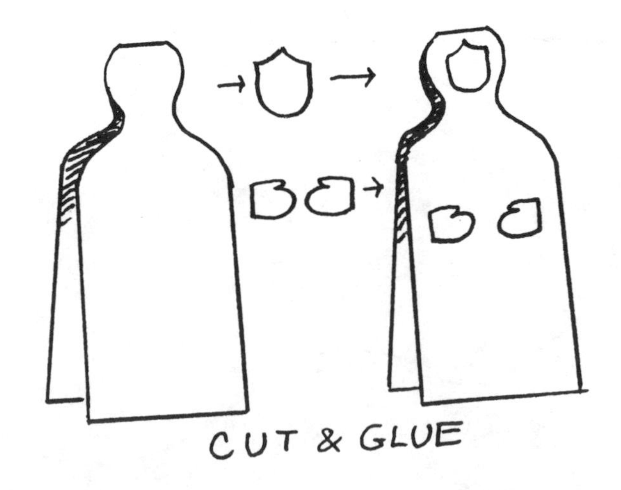

# Patterns for "The Road to Bethlehem"

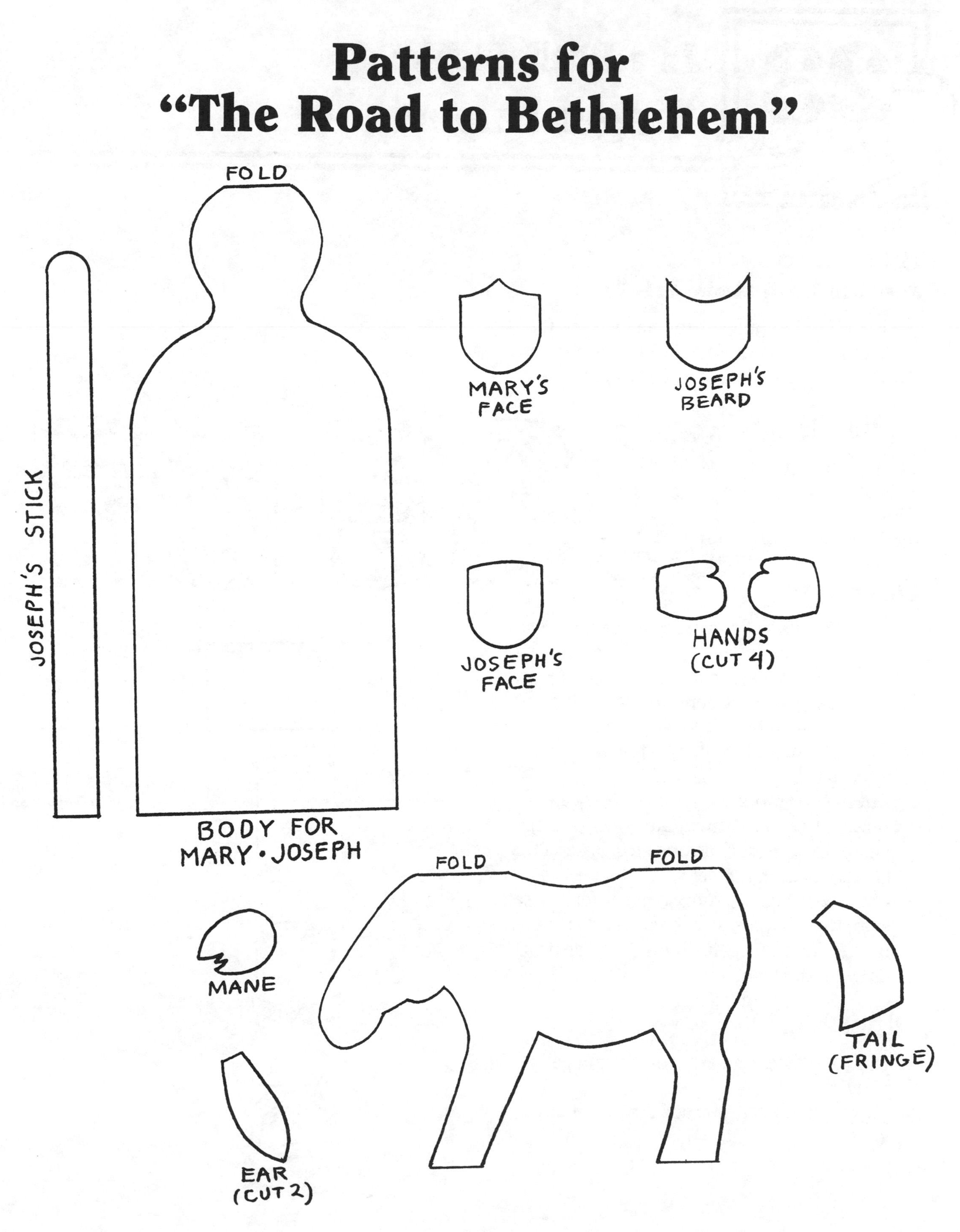

# In a Little Stable: Finger Puppets

## Bible Story

**Jesus Is Born (Luke 2:1–7)**

Use the finger puppets to help you tell the story of Jesus' birth. When not in use, set out the puppets for a Christmas decoration.

## Materials

Construction paper
Scissors
Glue
Markers (*optional*)

## Directions

1. Choose colors of construction paper to use to make each finger puppet. Make a puppet for Mary, Joseph, Jesus, a sheep, and a cow.
2. From each sheet of construction paper, cut a rectangle to fit around your finger. Glue the edges of each rectangle together to make a tube.
3. Cut narrow strips for arms for Mary and Joseph. Cut four hands. Glue one to each end of the strips. Glue one strip around the bottom of each puppet.
4. Cut pieces of construction paper for a nose, eyes, mouth, hair, and other details for each figure. Glue the features on the puppets. Or draw on the features.

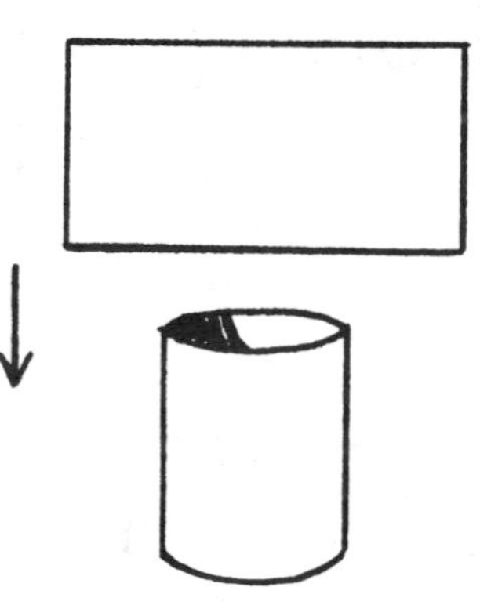

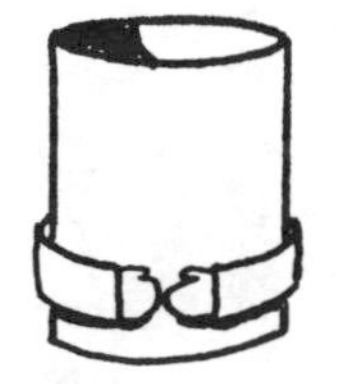

## Other Ideas

1. Draw the faces and arms on the puppet's body.
2. Make a stable out of a box and use it as a stage.

# Angels We Have Heard on High: Angel Garland

## Bible Story

### Angels Appear to the Shepherds (Luke 2:8–20)

What a sight the shepherds saw the night Jesus was born as a choir of angels filled the sky with music and light! Make your own choir of angels to decorate your Christmas tree.

## Materials

White paper
Scissors
Pencil
Glitter pen
Tape

## Directions

1. If needed, duplicate and cut out the pattern on this page.
2. Cut strips of white paper about 3″ wide.
3. Accordion-fold the paper (back and forth).
4. Trace around the angel pattern on the front fold of the paper. Make sure its shape extends to each fold.
5. Cut out the angels, taking care not to cut off the folded edges.
6. Unfold the angels. Use the glitter pen to dot on glitter.
7. Cut more angels. Connect them with tape.
8. Drape the angels around your Christmas tree.

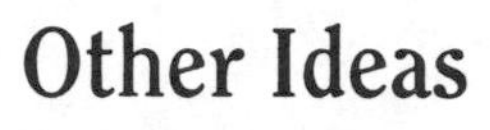

## Other Ideas

1. Cut angels from metallic foil or decorative wrapping paper.
2. Use glue and glitter instead of a glitter pen.
3. Use thin wire or thread to tie individual angels to a metallic garland.
4. Cut a different pattern for each week of Advent. Ideas include a star, bell, candle, crown, and manger.

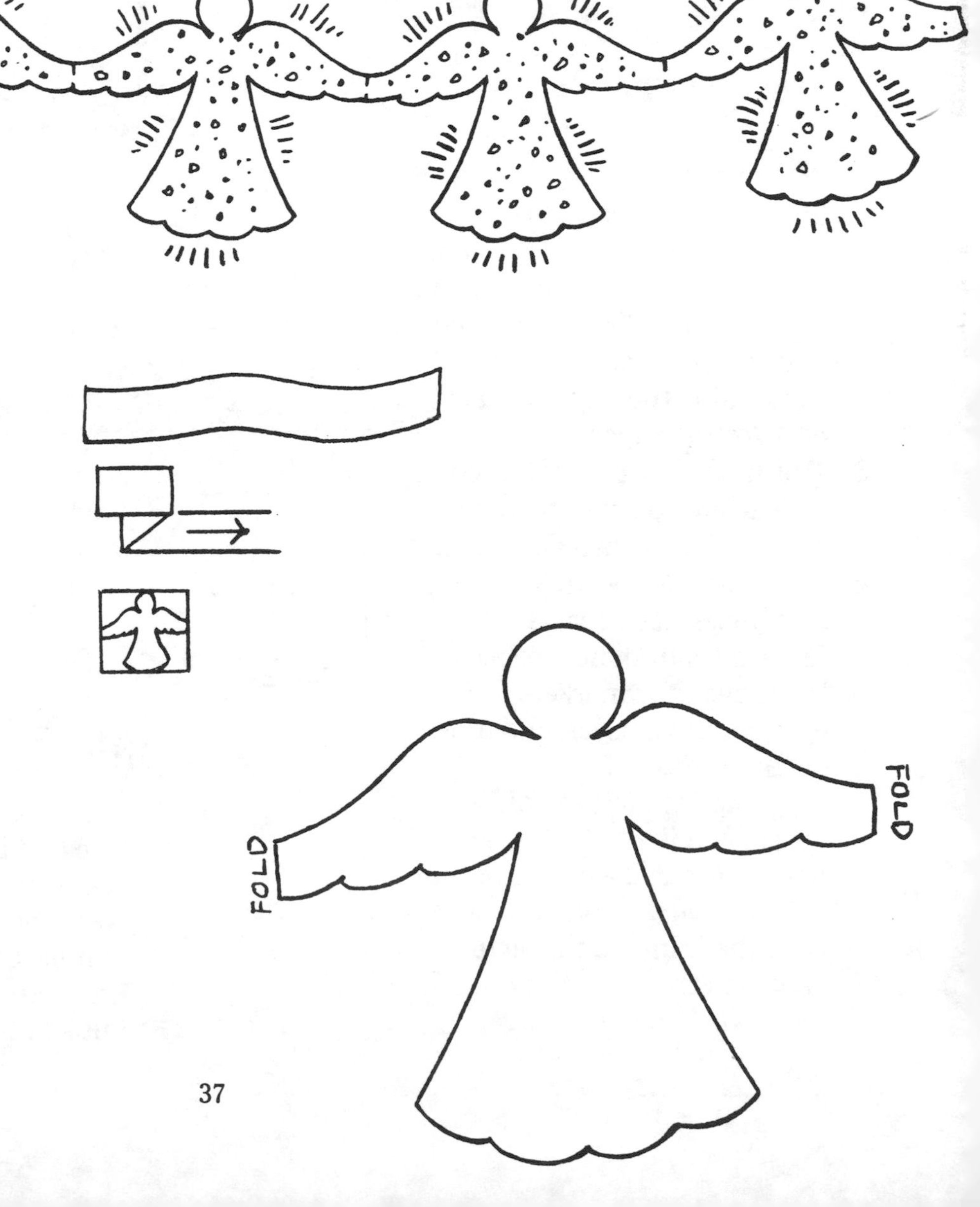

# 25 I Have Seen Your Salvation: Torn-Paper Collage

## Bible Story

**Presentation of Jesus (Luke 2:21–38)**

Simeon rejoiced to see Jesus, his salvation. Make a torn-paper collage to remind you that Jesus came to be your Savior too.

## Materials

Construction paper
Glue
Newspaper
Crayons or markers

## Directions

1. Choose a piece of construction paper to use for a background.
2. Carefully tear a face for Simeon and a face for Baby Jesus from flesh-colored construction paper. Glue the faces on the background paper.
3. Tear the upper part of Simeon's body from a colored piece of construction paper. Glue it on.
4. Tear hair and a beard for Simeon from newspaper. Tear Baby Jesus' body from newspaper.
5. Use crayons or markers to add eyes, mouths, noses, and other details as desired.
6. To frame the picture, fold a piece of construction paper in half. Tear out the center of the paper, leaving 1″ on every side. Glue the frame to the picture.
7. Write "I Have Seen Your Salvation" on the frame.

## Other Ideas

1. Write the whole song of Simeon on the picture (see Luke 2:29–32.)
2. Tear a speech balloon from white paper. Write the song of Simeon on it.
3. Tear paper eyes and mouths for each figure.
4. Use construction paper instead of newspaper.
5. Cut all the shapes instead of tearing them.

# Star of Wonder:
# Shape Ornament

## Bible Story

**The Visit of the Wise Men**
**(Matthew 2:1–12)**

A bright light in the sky led the Wise Men to Jesus. You, too, have seen the light of Jesus' love and worship Him. Make star ornaments to put on your Christmas tree to celebrate Jesus' birth.

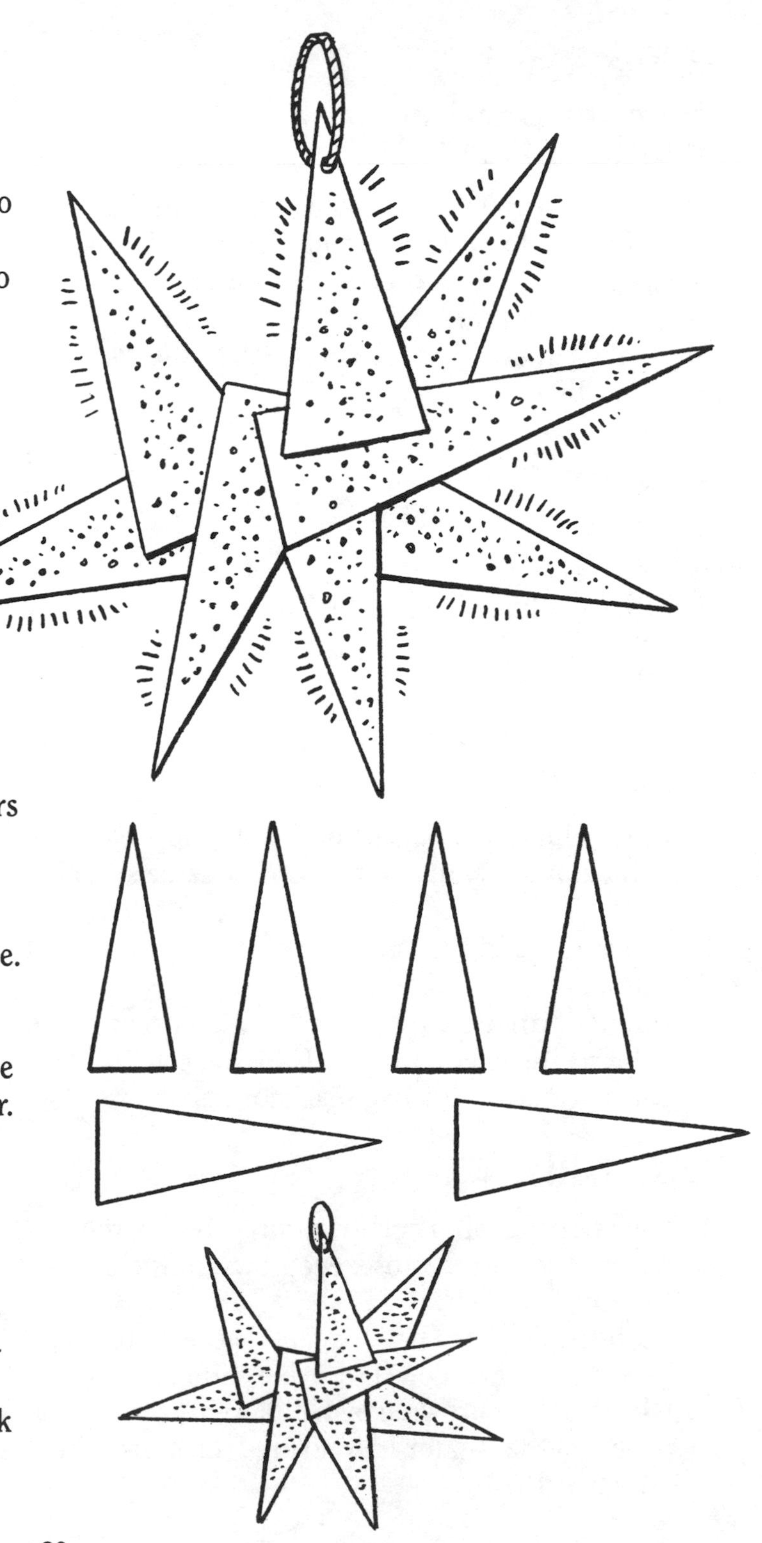

## Materials

Construction paper
Scissors
Glue
Glitter
Hole punch
Yarn or string

## Directions

1. Cut elongated triangles from different colors of construction paper. For fast cutting, fold the paper in half and cut two triangles at a time.
2. Arrange six or more triangles in a star shape. Glue them together.
3. Glue glitter on the star.
4. Punch a hole in one of the star triangles. Tie a piece of yarn through the hole as a hanger.

## Other Ideas

1. Use metallic paper instead of construction paper.
2. Make small stars for Christmas tree decorations and larger stars to hang from the ceiling.
3. Write "We Have Seen His Light" on the back of the star.

# Preparing the Way: Bag Mask

## Bible Story

**John the Baptizer (Matthew 3:1–12)**

More is written in the Bible about John than just his birth to Zechariah and Elizabeth. John the Baptizer was the forerunner of Jesus. God sent John to prepare the way for the Lord. Make a bag mask. Wear it as you tell the story of John's life.

## Materials

Large paper bag
Scissors
Tempera paint
Paintbrush
Construction paper
Glue

## Directions

1. Cut eyeholes in one side of a large paper bag.
2. Paint John's beard and face on the same side of the bag.
3. Cut a fringe in the open end of the bag to make his beard.
4. Cut and fringe strips of construction paper the same color as the painted beard. Glue the construction paper fringe on the bag mask for hair.

## Other Ideas

1. Glue flesh-colored construction paper on the mask for a face. Add a paper nose, eyebrows, mustache, and mouth.
2. Stuff the bag with newspaper. Tie the bottom of the bag to a wooden dowel to make a life-size puppet.
3. Glue black or brown construction paper or tissue paper on the bag for hair. Fringe the beard when the glue has dried.

# A Dove Came Down:
# Torn-Paper Mosaic

## Bible Story

**Jesus' Baptism (John 1:29–34)**

When Jesus was baptized, the Holy Spirit came down from heaven in the form of a dove. The Holy Spirit was also present at your Baptism. Make a torn-paper mosaic to remind you of this.

## Materials

Blue and white construction paper
Pencil
Glue
Markers or crayons

## Directions

1. If needed, duplicate and cut out the pattern on page 42.
2. Lightly trace the pattern on a piece of blue construction paper.
3. Tear white paper into small square and triangular shapes.
4. Glue the white paper inside the dove outline. Shapes may be overlapped or positioned with space between each piece.
5. Make a frame from a piece of white construction paper the same size as the blue construction paper. Fold it in half. Tear out the center, leaving a 1″ border. Glue the frame on the picture.
6. Write "A Dove Came Down" or similar words from the Bible story on the picture.

## Other Ideas

1. Write your name and the date of your Baptism on the picture.
2. Draw an outline of the dove on white paper. Fill in the background with pieces torn from blue paper. Or trace the dove on light blue construction paper and fill in the background with dark blue pieces.
3. Glue pieces of red paper around a dove shape or inside an outline of a flame for a Pentecost picture.
4. Cut a dove shape from white paper. Cut the shape apart. Glue the pieces together, slightly pulled apart, on another sheet of paper.
5. Draw outlines of shapes from other Bible stories (heart, cross, flower, rainbow, boat, shield, butterfly). Fill them in with torn or cut pieces of paper.

# Pattern for "A Dove Came Down"

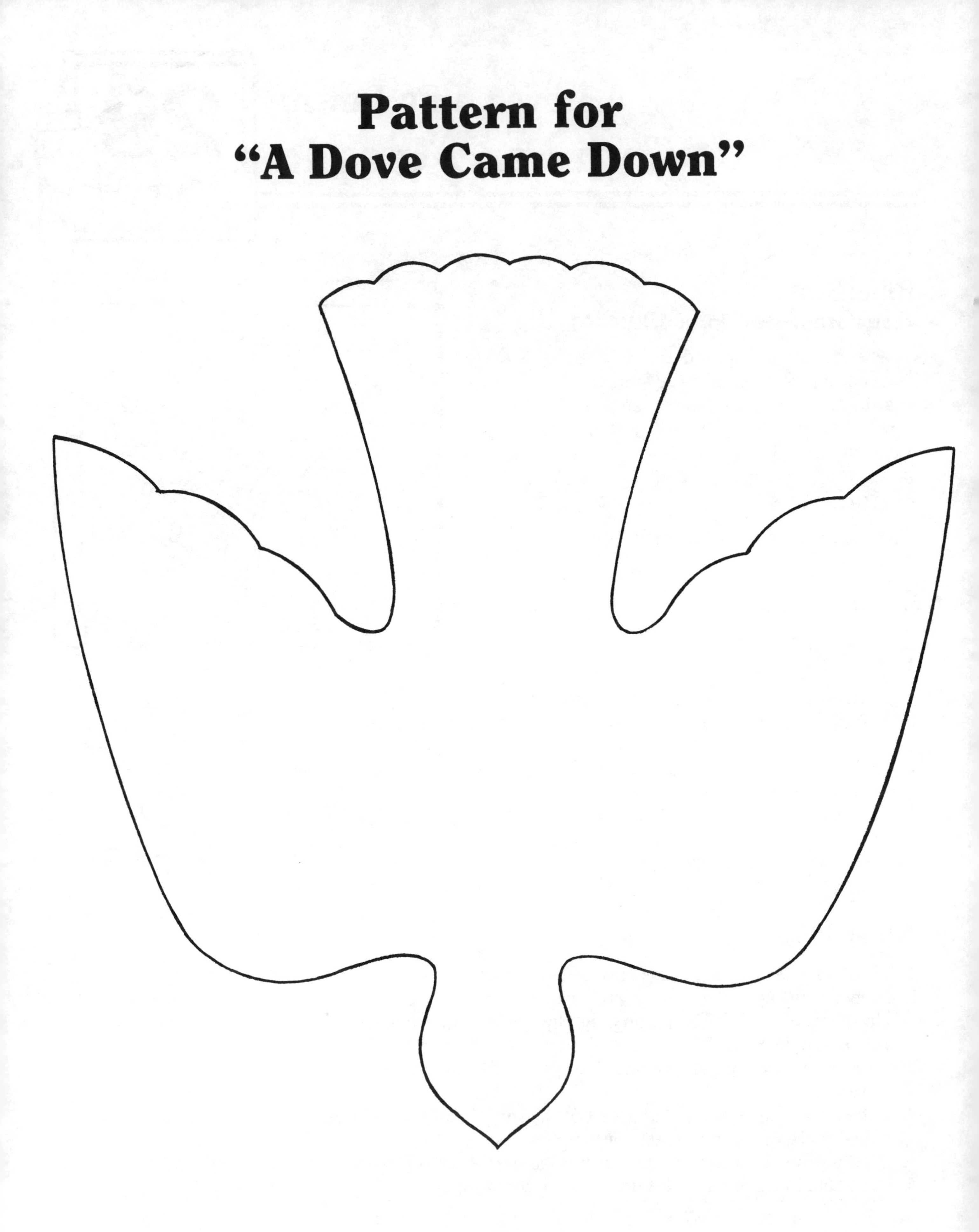

# God So Loved: Pull-Apart Collage

## Bible Story

**Jesus and Nicodemus (John 3:1–21)**

God so loved the world that He sent His only Son, Jesus, to save all people. Make a picture that reminds you that God loves you too.

## Materials

Red and white construction paper
Pencil
Scissors
Glue
Markers

## Directions

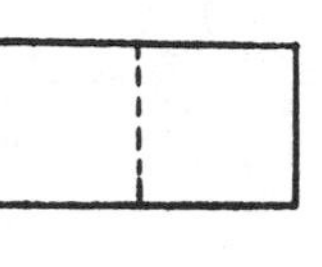

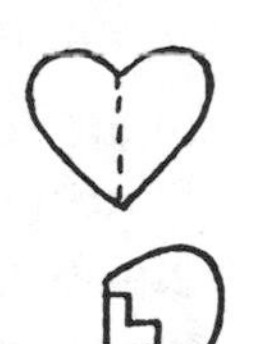

1. Fold a piece of red construction paper.
2. Lightly draw half a heart along the fold.
3. Cut out the heart.
4. Draw half a cross in the middle of the heart. Cut it out. Unfold the heart.
5. Cut the heart into puzzle pieces. (Younger children may only be able to handle a few pieces. Older children can work with more pieces.)
6. To avoid mixing pieces up, place them on a piece of white paper as soon as they are cut.
7. Glue the red heart pieces onto the white paper. Leave a little space between each piece.
8. Write "God So Loved (*name of child*)" on the picture.

## Other Ideas

1. Make this project but omit the cross in the center of the heart. Glue a picture of the child on the heart.
2. Use the heart picture to illustrate other lessons that emphasize God's love for us or the love He wants us to show others.
3. Use puzzle shapes to make Christmas, Easter, or get-well cards.

# Glow with God's Love: Paper Lantern

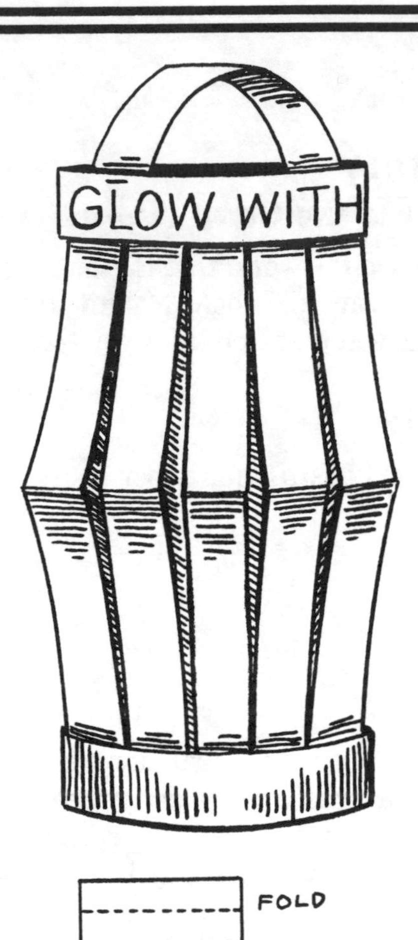


## Bible Reference

**You Are the Light of the World (Matthew 5:14–16)**

Like a light shining in the darkness, you are a light showing God's love in a world dark with sin. Make a paper lantern to remind you to let your Christian light shine to those you meet.

## Materials

Construction paper
Ruler
Pencil
Scissors
Marker
Glue
Stapler

## Directions

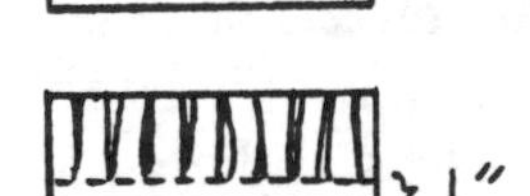


1. Fold a piece of construction paper lengthwise.
2. Use a ruler to lightly trace equidistant lines from the fold to a line 1″ from the bottom edge of the paper. Cut along the lines and unfold.
3. Cut 1″ strips from one or more colors to fit over the uncut paper at each end of the lantern.
4. Write "Glow with God's Love" on one of the strips.
5. Glue one strip to the top and one to the bottom of the lantern.
6. Roll the lantern into a tube and staple the edges.
7. Cut a strip of paper 1″ wide. Staple each side to the top of the lantern for a hanger.

## Other Ideas

1. Trim the lantern with ribbon or decorative fabric trim.
2. Fold out the paper strips in the center.
3. Glue bright tissue paper around the inside of the lantern.
4. Glue the lantern together instead of stapling it.
5. Tie a piece of yarn through two holes punched in the top of the lantern for a hanger.

# Just Say the Word: Paper Helmet

## Bible Story

**Jesus Heals the Centurion's Servant (Matthew 8:5–13)**

Make a paper helmet. Wear it as you tell the story of the Roman centurion and how Jesus healed his sick servant.

## Materials

Construction paper
Ruler
Pencil
Crayons
Scissors
Glue

## Directions

1. Use a pencil and ruler to draw three long, narrow strips, each about 2″ wide, on construction paper.
2. Use crayons to decorate the strips. Cut out the strips.
3. Glue the ends of one strip together to fit around your head. Add an extra piece to the strip, if needed.
4. Glue the second strip from front to back. Glue the third from side to side.
5. Cut two smaller strips for side flaps. Glue them in place.
6. Add other paper details and decorations as desired.

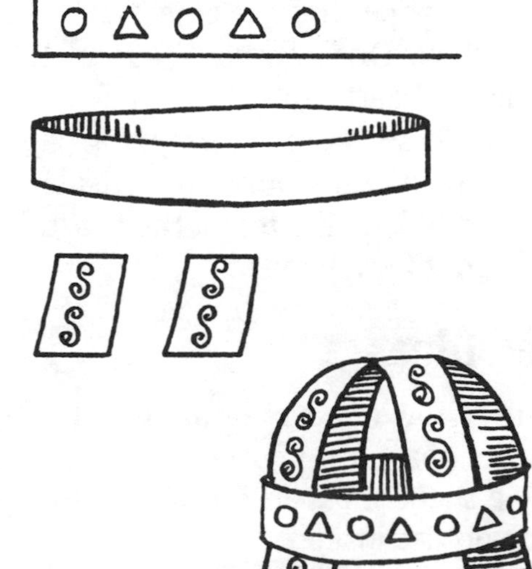

## Other Ideas

1. Use the helmet shape to make paper wigs or hats.
2. Wear the helmet as you tell about other soldiers in the Bible, such as Joshua or Gideon.

# Love One Another: Wrapping-Paper Collage

## Bible Story

**The Good Samaritan (Luke 10:25–37)**

Jesus told the story of the Good Samaritan to teach us how we are to show love to all people. Make a picture to remind you of how God helps you grow in love and show His love to those you meet.

## Materials

Construction paper
Scissors
Markers
Wrapping paper with flower design
Glue
Hole punch
Yarn

## Directions

1. Fold a piece of construction paper in half. Cut a half a heart along the fold. Open the paper to form a heart.
2. Write "Love One Another" (1 John 4:7) inside the heart.
3. Cut flower shapes from wrapping paper.
4. Glue the flowers around the outside edge of the heart.
5. Punch a hole at the top of the heart. Tie a piece of yarn through it for a hanger.

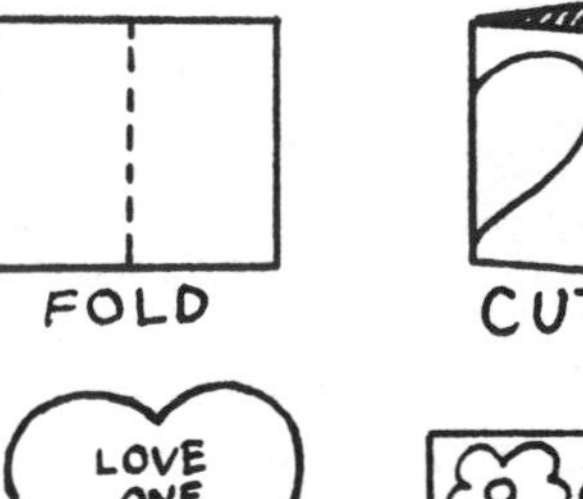

## Other Ideas

1. Write "Grow in Love" or another Bible phrase inside the heart.
2. Cut the heart from poster board. Decorate both sides. Hang it as a mobile. Make one for a friend.
3. Fold a sheet of paper to make a card. Glue flowers on the front and write an appropriate Bible verse on the inside.
4. Cut shapes other than flowers to go with a different emphasis (cross, butterfly, dove, sunshine).

# God Cares for Me: Flower Garden

## Bible Story

**God Cares for the Flowers (Matthew 6:28–34)**

Make a paper flower garden as a reminder that God, who cares for the flowers, also cares for you.

## Materials

| | |
|---|---|
| Construction paper | Scissors |
| Pencil | Stapler |
| Ruler | Markers |
| | Glue |

## Directions

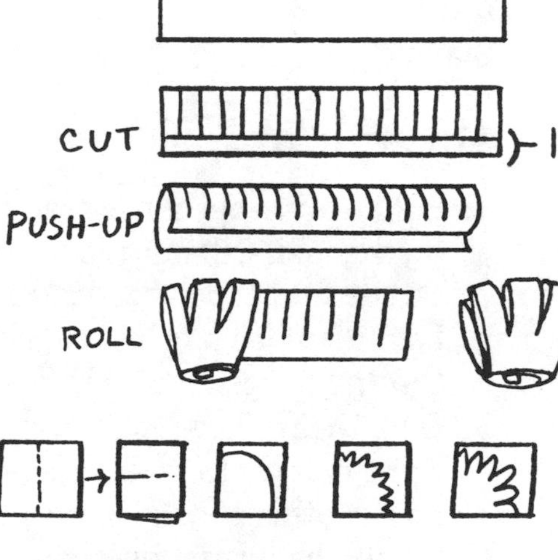


1. Fold a piece of green construction paper in half lengthwise.
2. Draw a line 1″ from the unfolded edge.
3. Cut a fringe along the folded edge. The cuts should be ½″ to 1″ apart and should not extend beyond the drawn line.
4. Push up one edge of the paper ½″ to 1″. Roll the fringed paper. Staple it together at the bottom to make grass.
5. Write "God Cares for Me" around the bottom of the grass.
6. Cut colored construction paper into 2″ (or larger) squares.
7. Fold each square in half. Fold it again. Cut a flower pattern in each square.
8. Cut circles from construction paper. Fold the circles in half three times. Cut flower patterns.
9. Cut small circles from several pieces of yellow construction paper placed together.
10. Glue different flower shapes together to make a flower. Glue a small yellow circle in the center of each flower.
11. Glue the flowers to the grass.

## Other Ideas

1. Glue single paper flowers onto the rolled green strip.
2. Use gummed circles for flowers. Or use flower stickers.
3. Cut heart-shaped flowers to glue to the grass. Use this project for lessons that emphasize growing in our love of God and of our brothers and sisters.
4. Cut flowers from tissue paper, metallic paper, or decorative wrapping paper.

# Jesus Loves Me: Stuffed Pillow

## Bible Story

**Jesus and the Children (Mark 10:13–16)**

Make a stuffed heart pillow to put in your room as a reminder that Jesus, who loved the little children and welcomed them to Himself, also loves you and is with you today.

## Materials

Newspaper
Pencil
Scissors
Glue
Markers
Stapler

## Directions

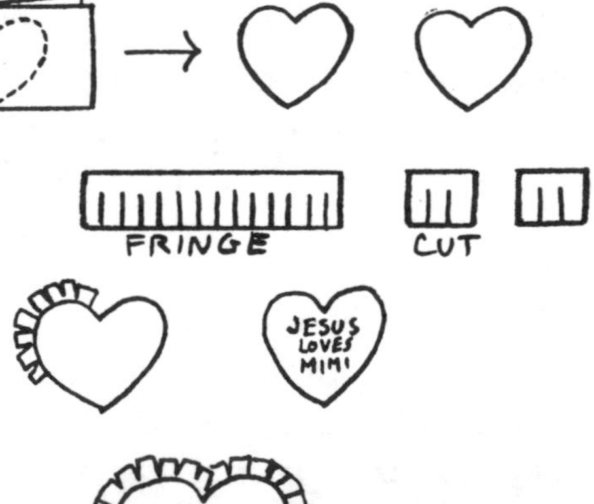


1. Fold two sheets of newspaper in half. Sketch a heart on the fold. Cut out the heart.
2. Cut several equal-sized strips of newspaper. Lay them in a pile and fringe them. Cut the fringed pieces into 4″ to 5″ sections.
3. Glue the fringed sections around one newspaper heart.
4. Use a marker to write "Jesus loves (*your name*)" on the other heart.
5. Staple the hearts together. Leave an opening for stuffing.
6. Crumple up small pieces of newspaper. Stuff the heart. When finished, staple the heart closed.

## Other Ideas

1. Use colored wrapping paper or poster board for the heart. Trim with pieces of construction paper.
2. Cut and glue on letters instead of writing "Jesus Loves *(name)*."
3. Write your friend's name on the pillow after the words "Jesus Loves." Give the pillow to your friend.
4. Make the pillow for another Bible story that emphasizes either the love of God for us or the love He helps us show to others.

# The Harvest Is Ready: Series Cutting

## Bible Story

**Jesus Sends Out the Disciples (Luke 10:1–24)**

Cut a series of wheat shafts and heads of grain for a picture that will remind you of the many people who await the Good News that Jesus died and rose for them.

## Materials

Blue and yellow construction paper
Scissors
Pencil
Glue
Markers

## Directions

1. If needed, duplicate and cut out the pattern on this page.
2. Cut a strip of blue construction paper. Cut a yellow piece of construction paper 1½" more in length and width for a background paper.
3. Fold the blue paper into narrow accordion strips (back and forth).
4. Trace the wheat shaft and head of grain along the folded side of the paper. Cut it out.
5. Unfold the blue paper to reveal a series of wheat shafts. Center and glue it onto the yellow sheet.
6. Write "The Harvest Is Ready" on the picture.

## Other Ideas

1. Use yellow tissue paper and black construction paper or poster board. Hang it as a sun catcher.
2. Substitute another design for another Bible passage
3. Cut the stalks into a folded paper circle.

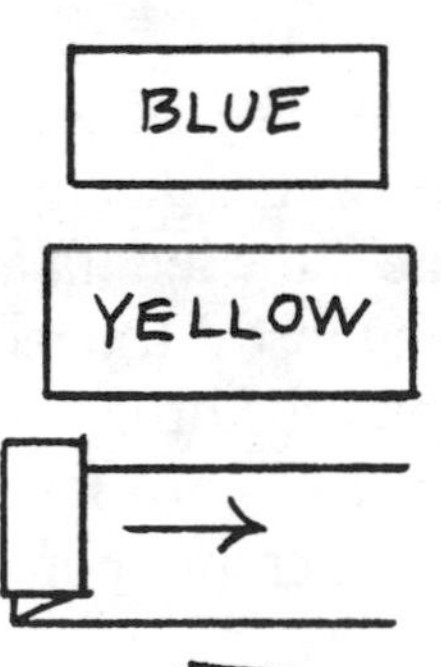

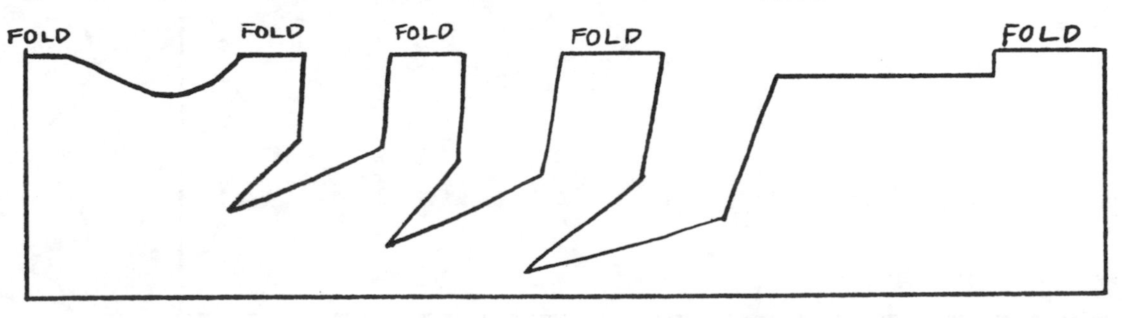

# 36 Alive in the Lord: Pop-Up Figure

## Bible Story

**Jairus' Daughter (Luke 8:41–56)**

Jesus made a dead little girl alive again. Make a pop-up figure of the little girl and use it as you tell the story.

## Materials

Construction paper
Pencil
Crayons or markers
Scissors
Glue

## Directions

1. If needed, duplicate and cut out the patterns on this page.
2. Trace the pattern of the little girl on a piece of construction paper. Use crayons or markers to add her eyes, nose, mouth, hair, and other details. Cut her out.
3. Trace the rectangle for her bed. Make it long enough to fold up from the bottom and cover the girl up to her chin. Fold back the top ½″.
4. Cut a long rectangle the same length as the bed.
5. Accordion-fold (back and forth) the rectangular piece. Glue one piece to the back of the girl and the other to the inside of her bed.
6. Cover the girl inside the bed until Jesus brings her back to life. Then lift the cover and watch her pop up.

## Other Ideas

1. Cut a blanket for the girl's bed from wallpaper or wrapping paper.
2. Use pop-up figures to illustrate other Bible stories.

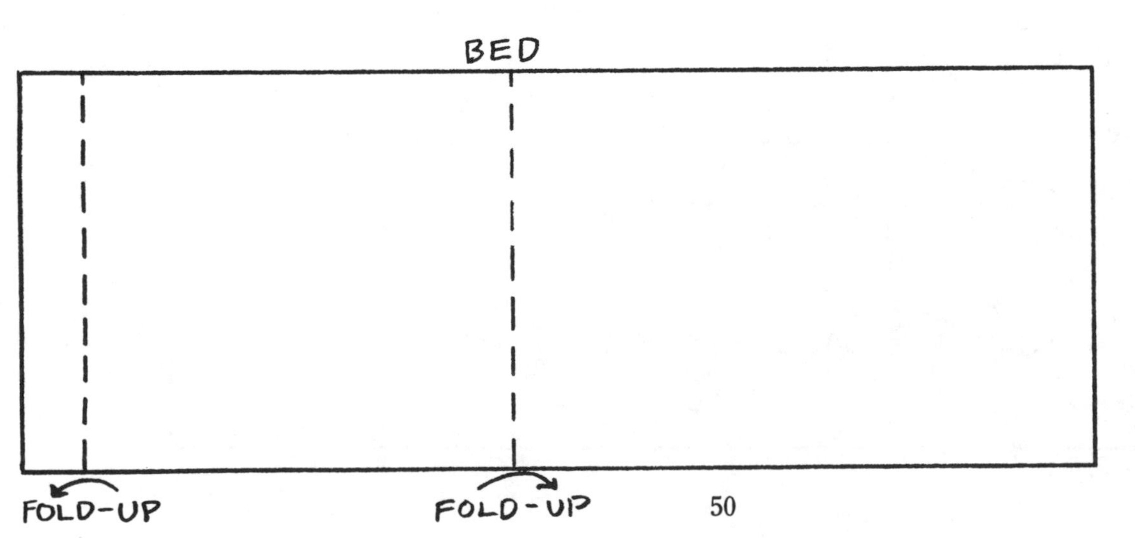

# See Me Move: Expandable Puppet

## Bible Story

**Jesus Heals a Paralyzed Man (Matthew 9:1–8)**

Make an expandable puppet. Use it as you tell the story of how Jesus made a paralyzed man walk again.

## Materials

Construction paper
Scissors
Pencil
Markers
Hole punch
Yarn

## Directions

1. If needed, duplicate and cut out the pattern on this page.
2. Fold a piece of construction paper in half. Trace the pattern on the fold. Cut it out.
3. Use a marker to add hair, facial features, and other details.
4. Fold the figure in half again. Cut lines from opposite directions, alternately, down the body of the figure.
5. Punch a hole in the top of the head. Cut a piece of yarn and tie it through the hole as a hanger.

## Other Ideas

1. Make the man's robe from wallpaper.
2. Glue a paper roll under the man's arm for his bed.

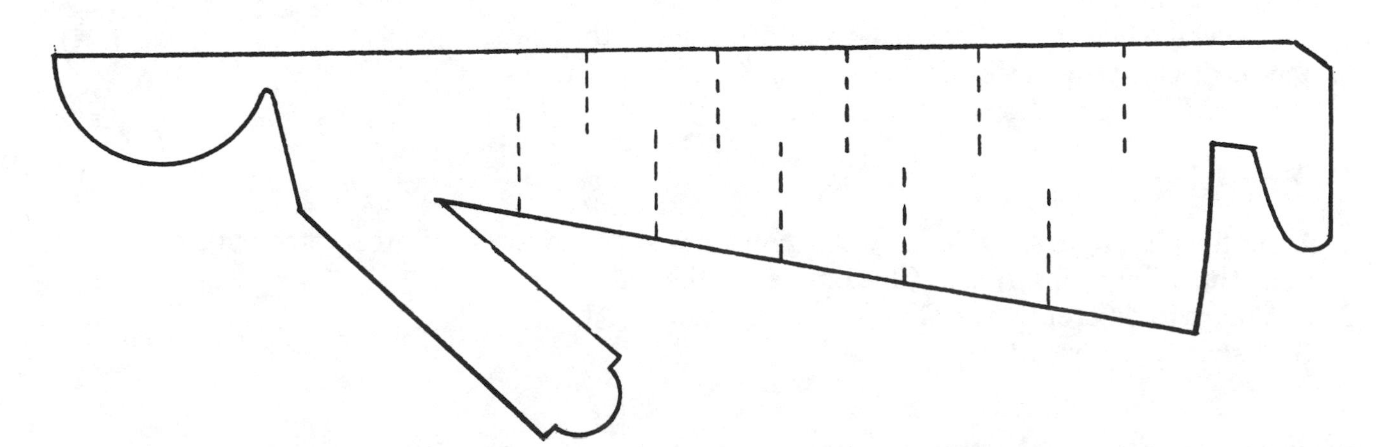

# Lord of the Wind and the Waves: Paper-Strip Collage

## Bible Story

**Jesus Stills the Storm (Luke 8:22–25)**

Glue strips of paper to make a picture of Jesus stopping the storm. Let it remind you that Jesus has power over everything, including storms and waves.

## Materials

Construction paper
Pencil
Ruler
Scissors
Transparent tape

## Directions

1. Choose a piece of construction paper for a background.
2. Choose construction paper to make the boat and waves.
3. Draw equidistant lines (about 1″ in width) on the different colors of paper. Cut them out. (To do multiple cuttings, draw lines on only one sheet, place other sheets under it, and cut all the layers at one time.)
4. Use the strips placed on edge to draw the picture. This will produce a 3-D effect. Outline the boat. Trim individual strips as needed. Use transparent tape to connect the pieces to each other and to the background paper.
5. Cut several white strips. Use them to outline Jesus in the boat.
6. Tape strips for water. Decide whether to picture the storm at its height or after Jesus tells it to stop.

## Other Ideas

1. Adapt the picture to show Jesus walking on the water or to show the great catch of fish.
2. Bend the paper strips in half. Glue one half to the page.
3. Cut strips in different sizes. Glue all the strips down flat.
4. Glue strips with craft glue.

# Lift High Your Palms:
# Fringed Paper

## Bible Story

**Jesus Enters Jerusalem (Matthew 21:1–11)**

Make a palm branch. Wave it as you sing "Hosanna," pretending to be part of the crowd who welcomed Jesus, our Savior-King, to Jerusalem.

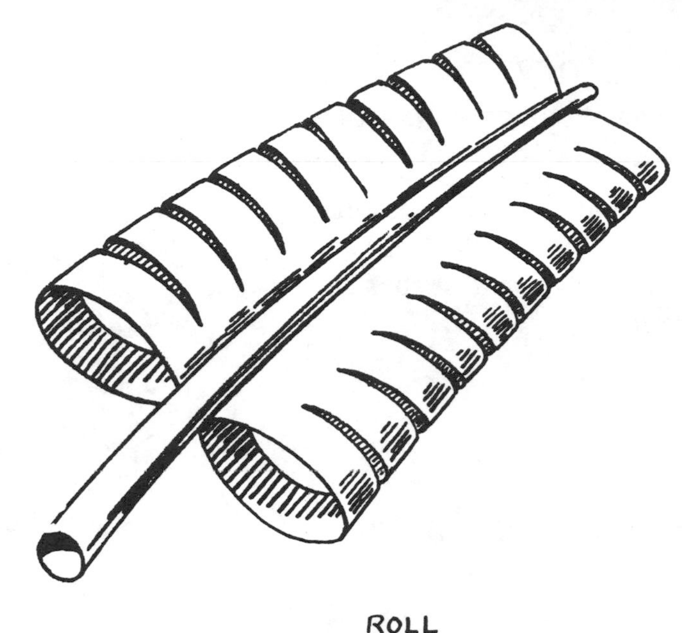

## Materials

Two pieces of green construction paper
Tape
Scissors
Ruler
Glue

## Directions

1. Roll one sheet of green construction paper lengthwise into a tube.
2. Tape the edges together.
3. Fold the other sheet in half lengthwise.
4. Cut 3″ from one end. (Vary the length according to the size of the children's hands.) Unfold.
5. Fold the two sides toward the middle so they overlap slightly at the center. Crease each side and glue it down.
6. Draw two parallel lines, 1″ apart, down the middle of the sheet.
7. Cut fringes ½″ to 1″ apart from the folded sides to the line.
8. Glue the paper tube down the center of the two sheets. Tape for stability.

## Other Ideas

1. Fold one sheet of green construction paper in half lengthwise. Cut the curved sides of a palm on the unfolded side. Then cut a fringe into the unfolded side to a line 1″ from the fold. Open. Glue a rolled tube down the center of the branch for stability.
2. Write "Hosanna" down the center of one side of the palm branch or along individual leaves.
3. Cut the palm branch from metallic green paper.

# Hosanna to the King: Mobile

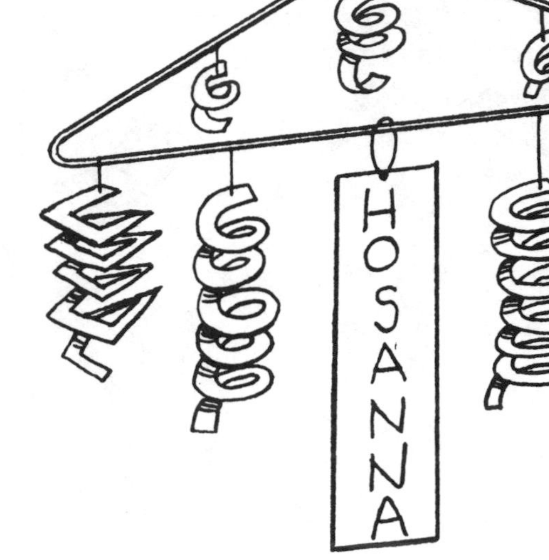


## Bible Story

**Children Praise Jesus in the Temple (Matthew 21:12–16)**

The children cried "Hosanna" to Jesus in the temple. Make a mobile from colorful shapes to praise Jesus today.

## Materials

Construction paper
Scissors
Markers
Hole punch
Yarn
Coat hanger
Glue

## Directions

1. Cut a strip of construction paper. Write "Hosanna" down the strip. Punch a hole at the top.
2. Cut the yarn into pieces of various lengths. Tie the "Hosanna" strip to the center of the hanger.
3. Make any combination of the following shapes to hang on the mobile. Punch a hole at the top of each one and tie it to the hanger with a piece of yarn.

**Spring**

a. Cut a circle or square.
b. Cut a continuous line to the center of the circle or square.

**Slash**

a. Cut a paper shape.
b. Cut several slashes into the shape.
c. Bend or fold the paper pieces back. Glue in place.

**Fold, Twist, and Curl**

a. Cut strips of paper.
b. Fold, curl, or twist paper into different shapes.
c. Glue together as desired.

## Other Ideas

1. Hang various shapes from a wooden dowel.
2. Add glitter to the shapes.
3. Cut shapes from metallic paper, wrapping paper, or poster board.

# Branches on the Vine:
# Paper-Sculpture Poster

## Bible Story

**Jesus Is the Vine (John 15:1–17)**

Jesus used a vine and its branches to tell how He keeps us connected to Him as we grow in faith. Make a paper-sculpture poster as a reminder of His words of promise.

## Materials

Green, brown, and blue construction paper
Scissors
Glue
Markers or crayons

## Directions

1. Cut a brown strip of paper for the main branch (Jesus). Cut smaller brown pieces for other branches. Glue them to the blue background paper.
2. Cut green leaves. Make multiple cuttings by cutting several layers of green paper at one time.
3. Score each leaf with the dull edge of a scissors blade to etch a line down the middle of each leaf. (Practice on another piece of construction paper until you can etch a good, firm line.)
4. Fold each leaf up on its scored line. Glue the scored part of the leaves onto the branches.
5. Write these words on the poster: "I am the vine; you are the branches" (John 15:5).

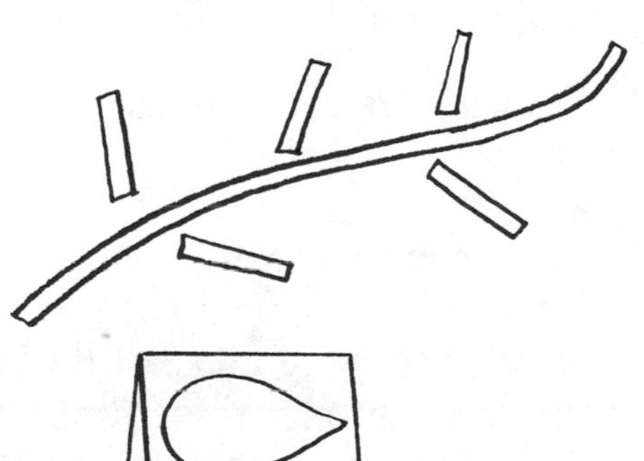

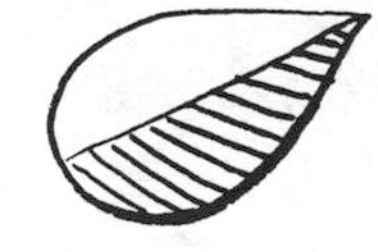

## Other Ideas

1. Score enough leaves to make a tree. Use this project for the story of Zacchaeus or for Psalm 1.
2. Glue leaves flat on the paper.
3. Add coiled grapes. Use this project for the lesson of the spies sent to the Promised Land (see Numbers 13:16–25).

# Jesus Died for Me: Pull-Apart Collage

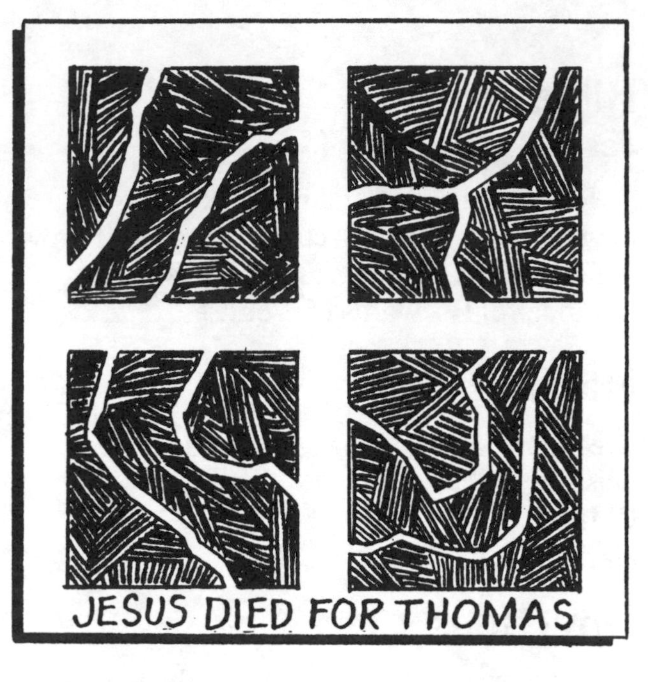


## Bible Story

**Jesus Died on the Cross (John 19:17–37)**

Make a pull-apart collage to remind you that Jesus died for your sins and secured eternal life for you.

## Materials

Purple and black construction paper
Scissors
Pencil
Markers

## Directions

1. Cut a square of black paper.
2. Lightly draw two lines on the paper to make a cross.
3. Cut the paper apart.
4. Place these four smaller squares on a piece of purple paper. Pull apart the four squares to allow a purple cross to show between them. Glue down the squares. (Older children can cut additional lines through each square, pull them apart a little, then glue them down.)
5. Write "Jesus Died for (*name of child*)" across the bottom of the picture.

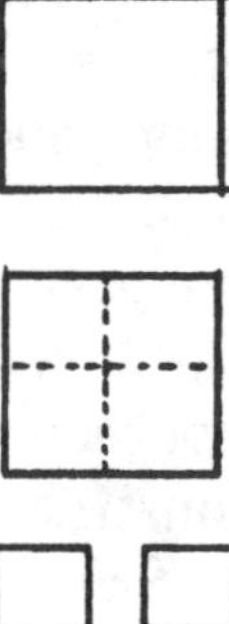

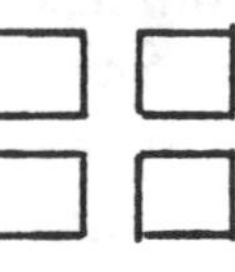

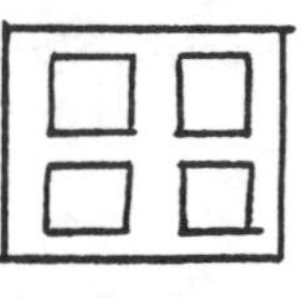

## Other Ideas

1. Have older children look up and write a Bible passage about Jesus' redeeming death on the cross on the bottom of the sheet.
2. Instead of cutting the cross shape, tear it.
3. Use large sheets of construction paper to make a poster. Glue the pull-apart black and purple cross onto a larger sheet of paper or poster board.

# Share the Joy:
# Three-Fold Easter Card

## Bible Story

**Jesus' Resurrection (Matthew 28:1–10)**

Jesus' friends shared their joy of His resurrection with others. Cut and fold an Easter card that you can give away to share your joy with others.

## Materials

White, grey, and yellow construction paper
Scissors
Envelope
Pencil
Markers

## Directions

1. Cut a strip of construction paper ¼″ narrower than the width of your envelope and at least ¼″ shorter than three times its length.
2. Accordion-fold the strip back and forth into thirds.
3. Sketch a Jerusalem skyline across the top of the three strips. Draw the skyline lowest on the first section and highest on the last. Add hills and trees on the third strip. Cut out the skyline.

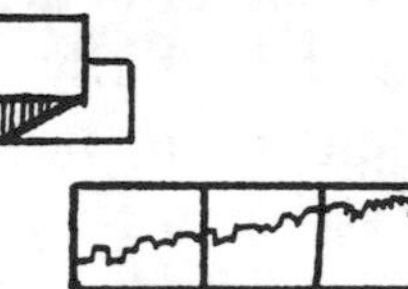

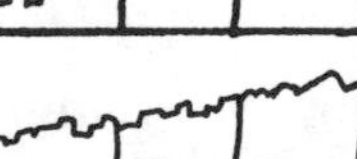

4. Cut a half-circle from gray paper. This is the tomb. Cut a circle for the stone. Glue these near the bottom of the last section.
5. Cut small yellow strips of paper. Glue them around the tomb for rays.
6. Write "He Is Risen" inside the open tomb.
7. Fold the card, sign it, put it in an envelope, and give it to a friend.

## Other Ideas

1. Draw the open tomb and stone with markers.
2. Fill the open tomb with yellow construction paper or metallic paper.
3. Write a Bible verse on the last fold.
4. Make a Christmas card by cutting a Bethlehem skyline. Add Jesus in the manger on the last section.

# Alleluia Mobile: Cutting on the Fold

## Bible Story

**Jesus Is Alive (Matthew 28:1–10)**

When the angel told Jesus' friends that He had risen from the dead, they were filled with great joy. Make an alleluia mobile to show your joy that Jesus, your best friend, is alive.

## Materials

Construction paper
Scissors
Pencil
Glue
Markers or crayons
String or thread

## Directions

1. If needed, duplicate and cut out the patterns on page 59.
2. Determine how many butterflies you want to make for your mobile. Cut construction paper into enough squares and rectangles for the number of butterflies you are making. Make different sizes and use different colors of paper.
3. Fold each piece of paper and draw one wing of a butterfly along the center fold. Cut out. Unfold the paper.
4. Cut out and glue on different-colored pieces of paper onto both sides of each butterfly.
5. Write the word "Alleluia" on one butterfly.
6. Cut a long piece of string or thread. Lay the butterflies in a row vertically and glue the string or thread down their center folds. Let dry.
7. Tie a loop at the top as a hanger.

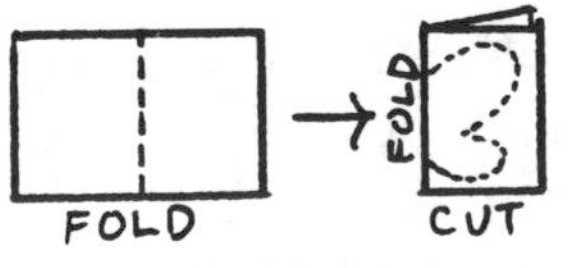

## Other Ideas

1. Write a Bible passage on one side of each butterfly.
2. Cut smaller butterfly shapes from different colors to glue inside the larger shapes.
3. Hang individual butterflies from a wooden dowel.
4. Connect butterflies by punching holes in the tops and bottoms, then tie them together with pieces of yarn.
5. Cut butterflies from wallpaper, metallic paper, or decorative wrapping paper.
6. Decorate butterflies with circle stickers, sequins (use craft glue), or glitter.
7. Fold several squares or rectangles of paper together to cut identical butterflies.
8. Cut holes in the wings and cover the holes with various colors of tissue paper.

# Patterns for "Alleluia Mobile"

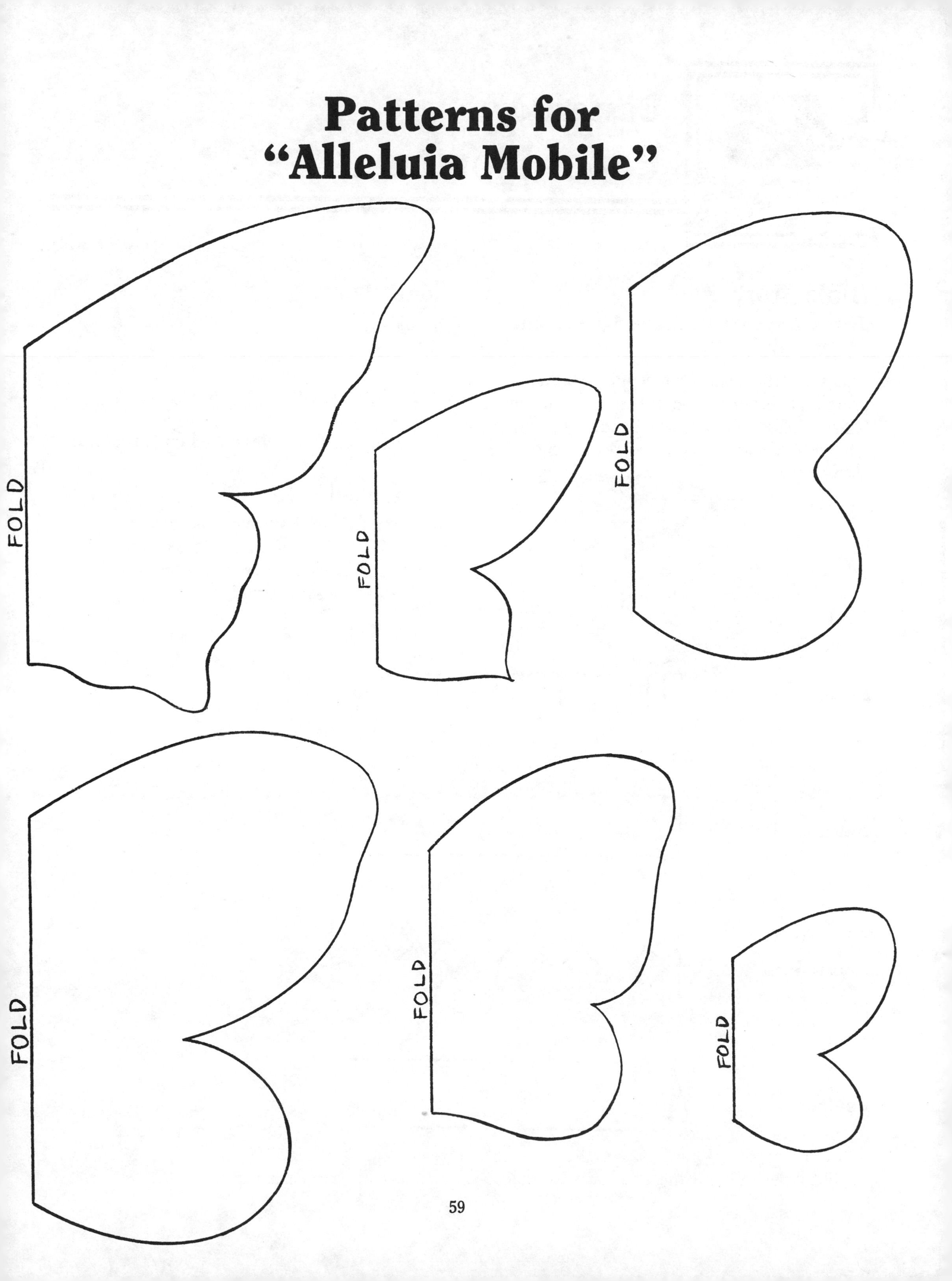

# Easter Joy:
# Paper Flowers

## Bible Story

**Jesus Appears to Mary Magdalene (John 20:1–18)**

Discuss the beautiful new life Jesus has given all believers through His saving actions. Make an Easter centerpiece to place on your table. Share your joy in Jesus' resurrection with others.

## Materials

Tissue paper
Scissors
Glue
Green florists' tape
Wire
Paper gift bag (see pages 63–64 for this project)

## Directions

1. Cut a strip of tissue paper according to the kind of flower you want to make. For faster cutting, place two strips together and cut both at the same time.

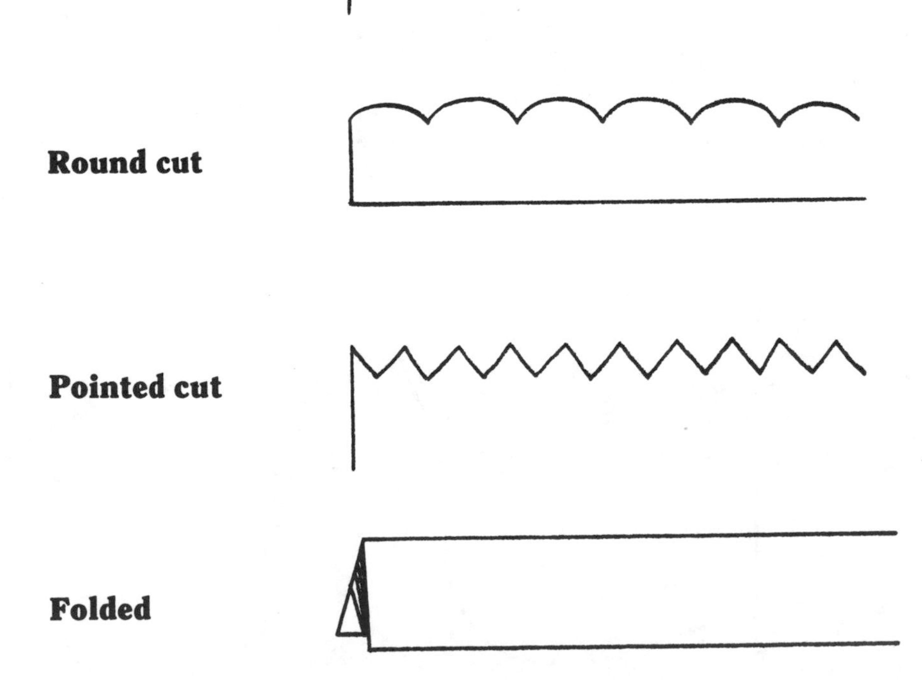

2. Start at one end of a strip and roll it up, gathering it at the bottom as you roll it. Twist and glue the tissue paper at the bottom, then add a second strip. Continue until your flower is the size you want to make it.
3. Use florists' tape to attach the flower to a piece of wire. Stretch the tape as you wrap. Wrap the wire with tape too.
4. Make the paper basket described on pages 63–64. Write the words "Easter Joy" on the basket. Add the flowers. Use this as a centerpiece or give it to someone as you share the joy of Jesus' resurrection.

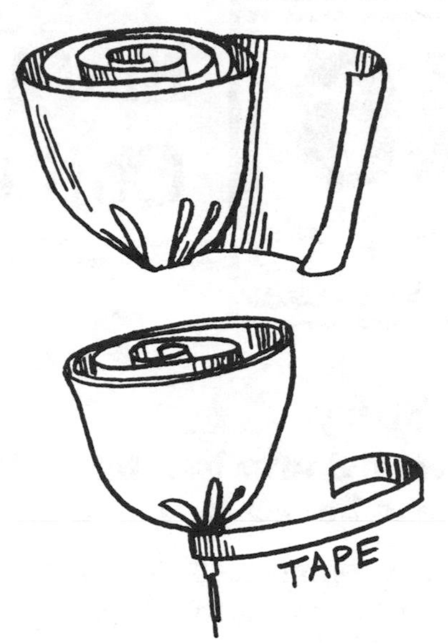

## Other Ideas

1. Crepe paper, paper twist, facial tissues, bond paper, construction paper, and metallic paper can also be used for flowers.
2. Tie a card with the words "Jesus Lives" to a bouquet or to one big flower.
3. Use flowers to illustrate God's care for the flowers of the field or a lesson on creation.
4. Attach appropriate Bible verses to the flowers and give them to someone who is sick or in a nursing home.
5. Let the children look through seed catalogs or flower books from the library to see the wonderful variety of flowers God created. Then try to duplicate with paper crafts some of the flowers.
6. Make nonrealistic "fantasy flowers" with a variety of petal colors and shapes.
7. Cut individual petals. Twist and glue them to the wire.
8. Write a Bible passage or words that relate to another Bible lesson on the outside of the bag.
9. Write "Easter Joy," or other words, on a piece of stiff paper to create a card. Punch a hole in the card and the bag; attach the two with yarn or ribbon.

# Into All the World: Coil Cross

## Bible Story

### The Great Commission (Matthew 28:16–20)

Jesus has commanded us to reach out to all nations with the Good News of His love. Make a coiled-paper cross to remind you to tell others about Jesus.

## Materials

Blue, green, and yellow construction paper
Ruler
Pencil
Scissors
Plastic lid
Permanent markers
Hole punch
Glue
Yarn

## Directions

1. Measure and cut construction paper into strips ½″ wide.
2. Use a permanent marker to draw a cross inside the plastic lid.
3. Punch a hole at the top of the cross.
4. Roll the paper strips tightly into coils. Glue the ends. Use yellow coils to fill the cross shape and blue and green coils for the background. Spread glue over the cross shape and glue down the yellow coils. Repeat for the background.
5. Cut a 6″ piece of yarn. Tie it through the top of the lid for a hanger.

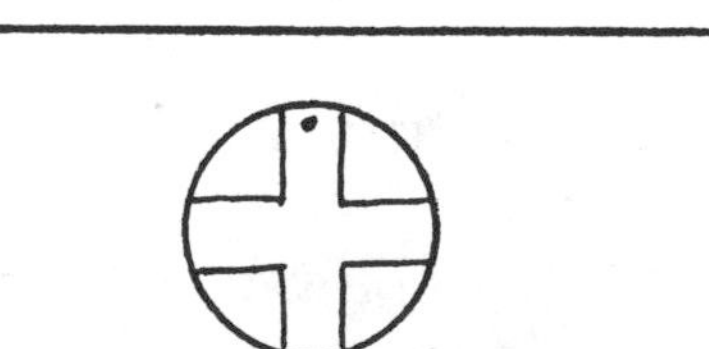

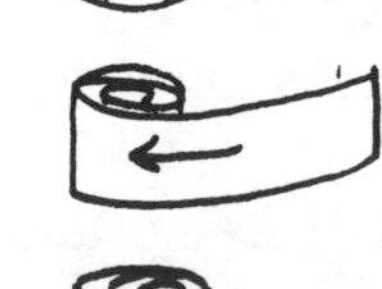

## Other Ideas

1. Use colored bond paper instead of construction paper.
2. Arrange the coiled paper inside a box lid.
3. Use coiled paper to illustrate scenes or themes from other Bible stories.
4. Make a coiled-paper world for a lesson on creation.
5. Cut paper strips ¾″ or wider.
6. Fit strips into a low, round, empty can. Cover the outside with a strip of paper with the words of the Great Commission written on it (see Matthew 28:19–20).

# A Gift of Love: Gift Bag

## Bible Story

**Dorcas Shows Her Love (Acts 9:36–42)**

Dorcas loved God. She showed her love as she helped people and sewed clothes for others. You can help other people too. Make a gift bag. Then put something special in it that you can give to someone.

## Materials

Wrapping paper
Pencil
Scissors
Markers
Construction paper
Hole punch
Glue

## Directions

1. Duplicate and cut out the pattern on page 64.
2. Trace the bag pattern on wrapping paper. Cut it out.
3. Choose a Bible passage. Write it on one side of the bag.
4. Punch holes from different colors of construction paper. Glue these to the sides of the bag.
5. Fold and glue the bag according to the directions.
6. Fill the bag with a gift for someone. (Suggestions: paper flowers, homemade candy, a snack mix, popped corn, a handmade picture or booklet with a Gospel message.)

## Other Ideas

1. Use wallpaper or construction paper to make the bag.
2. Make a bag to hold gifts for people who are shut-ins.
3. Use the bag to give a note or picture about Jesus' love to a friend.
4. Punch two holes on opposite sides of the bag. Tie yarn or ribbon through the holes to make a handle.
5. Write "God Loves You" on a piece of stiff paper. Punch a hole in the card and a hole in the bag; attach the card to the bag with yarn or ribbon.

# Pattern for "A Gift of Love"

**Directions**

1. Fold top flap in. Glue down.
2. Fold sides in.
3. Fold bottom side flaps up.
4. Glue bottom flap to bottom side flaps. Glue side flap inside the bag.

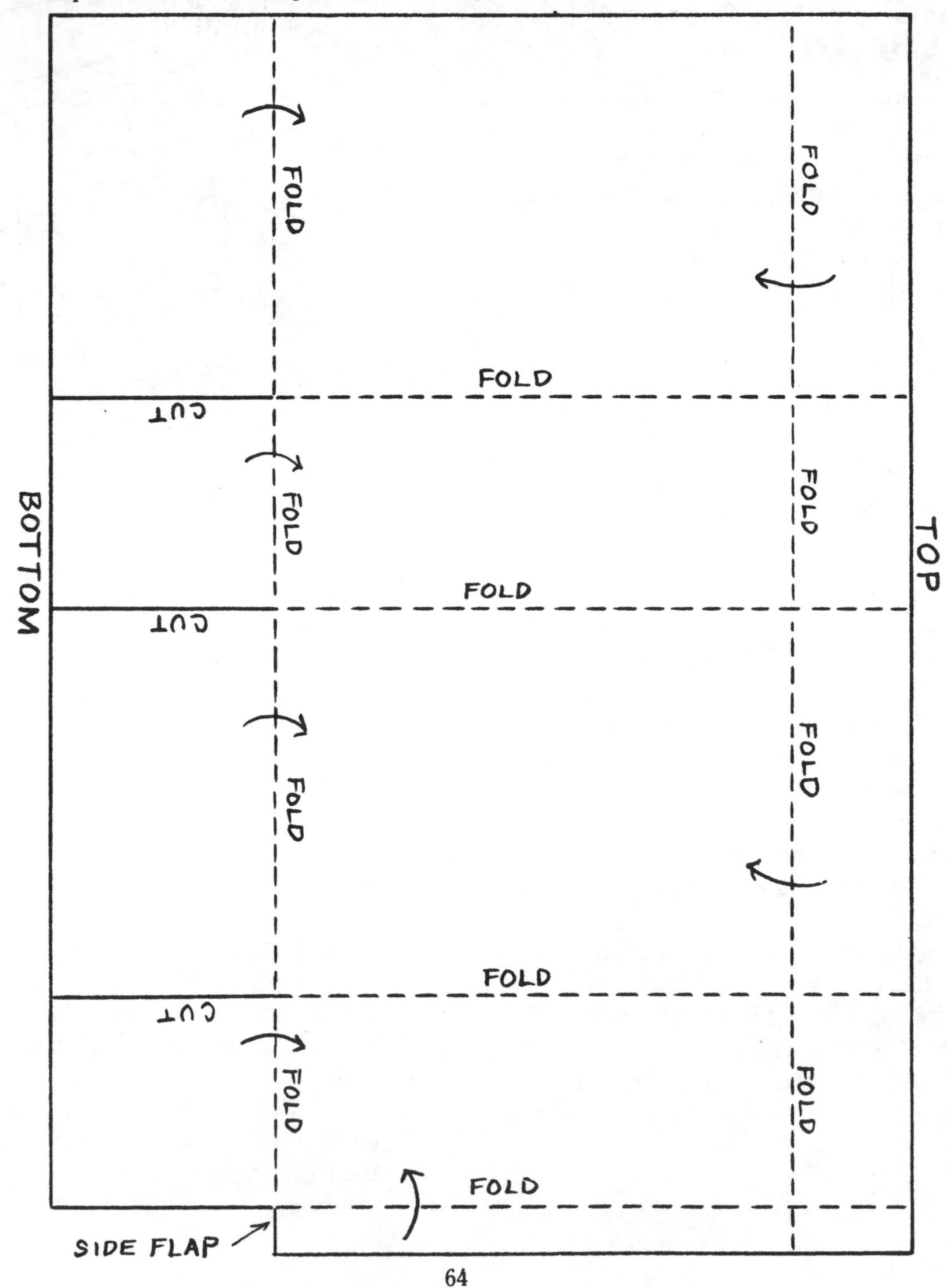